Is There More To Life Than We Know?

A Spiritual Journey and Awakening to finding God

Joseph LoBrutto III

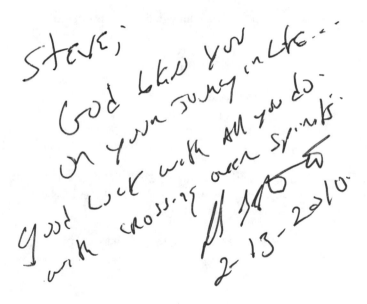

Steve;
God bless you
on your journey in life...
good luck with all you do
with crossing over spirits
2-13-2010

iUniverse, Inc.
New York   Bloomington

Is There More To Life Than We Know?

A Spiritual Journey and Awakening to finding God

iUniverse books may be ordered through booksellers or by contacting:

iUniverse
1663 Liberty Drive
Bloomington, IN 47403
www.iuniverse.com
1-800-Authors (1-800-288-4677)

ISBN: 978-0-595-43449-7 (pbk)
ISBN: 978-0-595-63284-8 (cloth)
ISBN: 978-0-595-87776-8 (ebk)

Printed in the United States of America

iUniverse rev. date: 11/04/2008

Table of Contents

Acknowledgements ....**xi**

Introductions ....**xv**

This journey begins when I was a child and had the gift of seeing spirits and concludes where I am now in my life; channeling the Collective, bringing God's wisdom, inspiration, healings and teachings to everyone. I have been called an extraordinary Psychic Medium; one who can connect you with your loved ones on the other side to bridge the gap between the earth plane and the spiritual plane of existence.

Journey of Life   **Chapter One** 1

When I was a child I had the special gift of seeing Spirits. An Irishman would appear with the surroundings of a rustic city behind him. He looked like a character right out of the Oliver Twist novel. He was a cheery fellow who always tried to amuse me. I would watch him try to juggle what looked like potatoes only to have them fall and roll all over the place.

The Brotherhood of Spirits   **Chapter Two** 11

The room was dark, but I noticed light escaping from under the door, which also somehow seeped through the doorframe. The door began to open and I felt a peaceful, loving, feeling of bliss as the rays of light passed through my body. What was this being of light?

The Great Spirit Chapter Three 27

The elder lived alone, away from his tribe. When he was traveling back to his home in the mountains, a fellow tribesman came to him and treated the elder with great respect as if he were chief. He begged the elder to return because his people knew that the elder was a shaman. The tribe was very much in need of a spiritual leader, in need of one who could talk to the Great Spirit.

Heaven Is Upon Us Chapter Four 35

"How can it be you, Rose? It has been twenty years since I last laid eyes on you. You look so young, so beautiful, like the day we married." "Yes, John it is I, Rose, and we are in heaven. You can create anything you want here. Just give it thought and it will happen. Feel the love of all the souls here. John, your soul is alive, it will live forever and yes, heaven is our home!"

The Sacred Fire Circle Chapter Five 43

I felt the heat of the fire and the beating of the drums shuddering through my body. The tribes spiritual leader jumped up on a pile of boulders surrounding the fire, raised his right arm towards the heaven as he held the prayer stick and called out, "Wakantanka," meaning Great Spirit.

The Secret Code Chapter Six 51

My eyes had been opened to the fact that we are not alone in the universe. I wondered if the influence of Deborah's description had clouded my thoughts. Out of the mist transpired a being with all the characteristics of an extraterrestrial. I could hardly believe what I had just seen.

Facing my Truths and Fears Chapter Seven 63

When God made the earth, it was made of beauty. Earth is known as the beacon in space for all souls to learn and grow spiritually. All physical substances of the earth are an illusion; your body of flesh is a part of that illusion. Your thoughts and your spiritual self are reality. When you leave this earth, you will shed the flesh that houses your spiritual self and will return to a state that is of pure thought and energy.

Promoter of God   **Chapter Eight** 69

"Joseph, you were a loyal follower, and friend to my brother Jesus. You had a caring heart and did all you could to help the people to understand who he was. You were a messenger of the Christ and now Joseph; you are to be a promoter of God. Your guides are the ones to help you prepare for a time when a Master will channel through you. A promoter of God! Yes, Joseph, this is your title on earth."

The Universal Life Force   **Chapter Nine** 75

As I was lying on the table, I felt a huge surge through my body. "Look! Joe's body is moving in all directions!" My shoulders started to lift off the table. It was as if someone was sitting on my back lifting my shoulder blades upwards. "What is going on now," my arms were being pulled backwards and then straight upwards to the ceiling. Jane explained to the class that spirit was giving me a universal healing.

Is Anyone Out There?   **Chapter Ten** 87

In an instant came a bright blinding flash as a white bearded man appeared sitting at a large wooden table where he was writing in some kind of tablet. When I approached the table, the man stood up to welcome me and that's when I recognized him. The vibration of the entity was powerful as it began to speak.

My Guardian Angel   **Chapter Eleven**....................... 97

If you need a description how we may look, you must eliminate the wings and halo. We are a non –physical being of a vibration of love and harmony. An aura of pure light surrounds our astral bodies. Our purpose is to serve the one and only God to deliver His love to everyone. We are to educate the beautiful people that are awakening on earth, so you are not alone!

Peace of Mind   **Chapter Twelve** 105

In the midst of my journey, I was led to the woman I was to marry. With the love and support of my wife, I have evolved into a fully developed medium. I was able to help her sister with the loss of their son. "I know how much you miss me and I can feel the pain of sorrow you carry everyday. It saddens me knowing that I cannot take the pain away. Please know that I will always be near. Life is really short and I want you to please live yours to the fullest."

Contacting the Departed   Chapter Thirteen 111

God granted me this gift to communicate with loved ones who have crossed over and it has given me great pleasure to help in the healing process for those who have lost someone. After the loss of a dear friend or loved one, we sometimes wish we could speak with them. Often times our loved ones will send us a sign to comfort us shortly after they depart. They don't want to scare us; they just want us to know that they are fine and still connected to us.

**Mama Always Said I was
Psychic**   Chapter Fourteen................. 121

As a Psychic I do not use any tools such as tarot cards, astrology or photos. I receive information by telepathy with my guides. In a reading I'm able to see opportunities and obstacles in your path whether it is in your past, present or future. When a client asks me a question, the Collective will take me back to the point in their past where the problem began.

Angels and Spirit Guides   Chapter Fifteen 135

My Guardian Angel informs the world of Lucifer and this legion of fallen angels. Angels have a hierarchy that oversees everything; they are known as the Archangels. God appointed these Angels in order to keep balance in the universe. The purpose in life of Angels and Spirit Guides is to bring forth the wisdom of God through messengers like me.

The Promise   Chapter Sixteen.................... 141

"Men call me Christ, but Christ is not a man. The Christ is universal love, and love is king. Look not unto your flesh, for it is not king. Look to the Christ, that is within, who shall be formed in every one of you, as it has been formed in me. I will return in spirit, one that is of light bodies, not flesh. Then you will witness the promise. The promise is of everlasting life given by God that your soul will live forever with the Father."

The New Age   Chapter Seventeen 163

For many years the beings of earth have lived without harmony. They wasted their life for wealth and power by invading and killing others for prejudicial reasons. There must be an end to this ego for it is destroying the true essence of your being-ness and what surrounds you. And so be it! As it was written at the end of this age, a New Age will occur. Yes, dear ones, this is the time we have been preparing you for, the merging of your higher self with your lower self, you are now one, you are now Self.

Different Faces and Places   **Chapter Eighteen** **169**

As the time comes near for the earth to change, there will be many UFO sightings. The strangers among you will purposely show themselves in order to make earth aware. There will be extraterrestrials in human form that will visit your earth, so please welcome them. We are not invaders of your home world. Our purpose is to help the inhabitants of the earth and to teach of the new laws of the universe.

The Ancient One   **Chapter Nineteen** **175**

The "I Am" is what I Am, All light bodies are all I Am, and everything that exists is I Am. The I Am is of love and harmony and it is of power and thought. The I Am is of you, me, and everything that is created. The universe is of one; and the one created all. The I Am is what I Am. Yes, Joseph, I Am that I Am! Remember these words and do not be afraid to use them. I Am God!

Acknowledgments

I would like to thank God and the Collective for the gift that has been bestowed on me. The wisdom of the Collective has been a wonderful influence on my life, for it has given me the ability to help people connect with loved ones in order to assure them that they are okay, and also to help those who have lost their direction in life find their journey's path.

To my loving wife; **Lisa,** having you in my life and sharing the same ultimate goals has brought us together on our journey's path. With your love, support, and continued sacrifices, I am able to continue to develop into a wonderful Psychic Medium. I would have never been able to publish this book with out your professional advice, patience, understanding, and of course, keeping me on my toes. I cannot begin to tell you that you are the world to me. I look forward to spending the rest of my life with you, making new memories and sharing our love.

I love you with all of my heart

I would like to include some acknowledgements of my family. First, I would like to thank my parents for teaching me loyalty and morality and for giving me love throughout my life; that has made me into the person that I am today. Dad, I look up to you as a role model of an ideal father. Mom, since I was a child you supported me with my spiritual work and I believe that I inherited the gift from your side of the family. I want to thank you both for believing in me and helping me to develop into a medium whose work comes from the heart.

*Thanks to my brother **Robert,** who is known as Uncle Rob to my kids. Thank you for treating all of my kids as if they were your own. As a young father my focus was on providing for my children and to make ends meet. You are a great uncle to my kids by keeping them entertained with your fun trips.*

To all of my children: I hope after reading this book, you will have a better understanding of what I have been doing all of my life.

__Todd,__ my oldest; you have become a wonderful father to Avery and Tyler. You have told me many times that you learned your parenting skills from me and that you would want to be the kind of father that I am. Well, you and Michelle are doing an excellent job raising my grandchildren.

__Adam,__ my middle son who is serving in the United States Navy; I am very proud of you and so is our country. You have grown into a substantial young man and one day will make an honorable husband and devoted father.

__Steven,__ the son of my wife Lisa and my youngest son - your mother and I are very proud of you as you pursue your goal of becoming a mechanical engineer. You have worked so hard in your studies. Knowing that you are a person of ambition and determination, I know that you will one day be a successful businessman when you finish college. Thank you for supporting me in my journey, for it means more to me than you will ever know.

*__Ashley,__ I fell in love with you the first time that we met. You were only five years old and you informed me that I had missed your birthday! You have grown into a caring mother to my granddaughter **Morgan.** Morgan reminds me so much of you as a child, beautiful and smart. Pop-pop loves you, Morgan!*

*My youngest daughter, **Jessica**; I guess you can say that your dad is not your ordinary father! But from the beginning you understood the gift that I had and we will always share this special bond between us. With the love and support you have given me, I have been able to practice channeling my guides. I love you very much and have watched you grow into a beautiful young woman. You have done so well in college and I look forward to watching you become a teacher in today's world to help sharpen the minds of the children. Lisa and I are so very proud of you and all of your accomplishments, especially of your award for **Women of Vision** from the city of Jacksonville, Florida. You are truly a role model to all young women.*

For all of the teachers on my journey's path, I would like to thank you for your time and devotion. Having the knowledge and sharing it with others reflects the prevalence of your mission to give of your gift back to God in loving kindness. In return, I hope the lessons that I have learned from you are expressed clearly and lovingly throughout this book. My wish for you is that all that you do in life brings you much joy and happiness.

And to my students thank you for your support and attention. Even though I was the teacher, I felt that I have learned a great deal from all of you. I would also like to give special thanks to two of my students; to Mary Collins, for your hard work and journalistic attentions to the manuscript to help me create an exciting book and to Maria Wheeler for all of the wonderful illustrations of my guides. It was fun to see them come to life under the power of your creative hand just as I have always seen them in my mind.

In loving memory of my Father in-law,
Douglas Murray.

May the afterlife be filled with Love
and Happiness.

May God always be with you on your
Never Ending Journey of Life.

Introduction

⌒⌒⌒◆⌒⌒⌒

We go to work to pay our bills, we raise our children, we try to take time for ourselves to enjoy life, but how much time do we take to wonder if there is more to life than what we know? How little time we spend on questions like "Why are we here on earth?" "Is there really a supreme being who created the universe?" "And why is life so hard, isn't there an easier way?"

Everyone is on his or her own journey of life. The people that we meet and the places we visit are all part of a plan to help us grow on our spiritual path. The lesson of life is what we learn everyday and in every way. We are learning new ways to get closer to God. Our loved ones who are with us on earth as well as those who have crossed over are part of the lesson. What is this lesson we're learning about? **To be one with God.**

As we live each day in our lives, we are learning new ways to get closer to God. Those of us who are on an enlightened path will see a change in our lives. **With age comes wisdom**. Look back a few years in your life and you will see how much you have grown. Things that once were very important to you are now not so important. The quest for spirituality is high on your list.

On NBC there is a comedy television show called "*My Name is Earl.*" It is based on Karma in a comical way. It reminded me of what I learned in Sunday school about the Golden Rule, "Do unto to others as you would have them do unto you." Wondering if the Golden Rule had anything to do with Karma, I looked it up in the dictionary and found that in the Hinduism and Buddhism beliefs, the word Karma means *the total effect of a person's actions and conduct during successive phases of his existence.* Another way to look at Karma, it stands for cause and effect. What goes around comes around and if you live by the Golden Rule, you should have good Karma.

Ever since I was a child, I was always interested in the unknown. I would sit up for hours gazing into the brightly lit starry sky wondering if we were the only life created by God or were there others like us? It's hard to imagine that earth is God's only creation since the universe is huge! Over the years I have become a real Sci-Fi nut, enjoying shows like *Star Trek, Star Gate,* and many others. Have you ever given thought on Extraterrestrials and UFO's? Before you dismiss the idea, think about the size of our universe.

It's hard to imagine that earth is God's only creation. Have aliens ever visited the earth? In Peru, the drawings made on top of the earth were made thousands of years ago. One of the drawings represents what appears to be an astronaut. These drawings can only be seen by air. Why were these drawings made? Could it be that the Peruvian met with extraterrestrials?

The topic of the supernatural is becoming more popular than ever. Everyone is so curious about the unknown. And the media just love to promote this subject these days. Shows like *Ghost Whisperer, Medium* and *John Edwards Crossing Over* are being aired everywhere. In *Ghost Whisperer,* Melinda Gordon, played by Jennifer Love Hewitt, communicates with earthbound spirits (ghosts who cling to the living because they have unfinished business that prevents them from moving beyond the familiar plane of existence that we call life).

Personally I think being able to see spirits is so cool! I can really relate to what she does. When I was a child, I, too, had the gift of seeing earth-bound and spiritual beings, but it frightened me. My parents thought I just had a very active imagination. I wish that when I was growing up I had a family member who could have explained to me that the spirits were real and to befriend them. This would have made me realize that what I experienced was real and I wasn't going crazy.

Today I take over where Melinda Gordon finishes. When the spirit goes into the light, she is finished with her job and this is where I begin. Like John Edwards in *Crossing Over,* I can communicate with the spirits who have crossed over into the light. We are called Psychic Mediums and our purpose is not for fortune telling, but we hold sessions to provide evidence that our loved ones live on after death.

The best part of my gift as a psychic medium is that I get to connect with spiritual beings that are masters and teachers to help with a person's spiritual growth in finding God. Using the psychic side of my abilities to help someone with their direction in life gives me great satisfaction.

The story you're about to read is a true story. It is about my own never-ending journey of life. This journey begins when I, as a child I had the gift of seeing spirits and continues to this time in my life as a channel for a band of Spirit Guides whom I call the Collective. As a channel, I am privileged to be able to bring God's wisdom, inspiration, healings and teachings to everyone. I have been commended as a Psychic Medium with extraordinary gifts who, by connecting you with your loved ones on the other side, can bridge the gap between the earth and the spiritual plane of existence. When I work with an individual, I help them to achieve a deeper understanding of the events in your life. I help people gain meaningful insights and give practical advice for their life. People will receive universal healings, support and guidance from the Collective.

While reading, *"Is There More To Life Than What We Know,"* you will sense the presence of "The Collective" and feel that you are a part of this incredible journey. You may find that parts of this story and the lessons taught to me may relate to your own personal journey of life. The majority of this book is channeled. For those who are new to channeling, you will have a better understanding by the end of the first chapter as to what it really entails. Remember to have an open mind and ask yourself if, just maybe, this could be true. Listen to your inner voice, and you might hear a "yes"!

Welcome to Our Journey in Life

Journey of Life

Chapter One

Childhood Visions

When I look back at my life I can see the foundation of events for how my life was to be. It started when I was a child; back then I had the special gift of seeing spirits. My childhood visions were a common occurrence for me.

One of the spirits I could see was a Native American. First I would hear the beating of drums in the distance and as I listened, the drums came closer and louder. Out of nowhere, the figure of the Native American would appear. He was a tall man with long flowing hair and appeared to have the strength of ten bears. He looked proud, like a warrior. When he visited, the Native American would bring his environment with him. We would see the bear cubs playing in the stream or a wolf pack on the hunt. Sometimes we would materialize together on top of a mountain and talk while looking over the beauty of the earth. It was as if I were being taken back in time to when the earth was young and pure. I watched as he played his drum, singing to the

1

heavens. He would point his finger to the sky and a ring of smoke would appear. The smoke ring would float around and encircle me. I now know that the ring of smoke represented the Circle of Life.

There were other spirits that visited me as a child as well. One that I recall quite vividly was the Irishman who would appear to me like a dream floating in the air with the surroundings of a rustic city behind him. He looked like a character right out of Dickens' *Oliver Twist*. The Irishman appeared to stand around five feet tall with curly hair that protruded from under what looked like an old shabby top hat. He wore a long-sleeved shirt with suspenders that crossed in the front and held a small pouch for bills under his arm. I could tell he was a jokester by the way he laughed as he tipped his hat towards me. He was a cheery fellow who always tried to amuse me. I would watch him try to juggle what looked like potatoes, only to have them fall and roll all over the place. I was surprised that my parents did not hear him, or me, laughing so hard!

Also, there was the man who looked to me like someone from early Biblical times. He was dressed in an ancient gray-colored robe and he carried what looked to be a manuscript. He was weather-beaten, with a white beard. He looked as though he had lived a very hard life, but a fulfilling one because he had mystical glow that surrounded his body. Every time I would see this man, he would be in a hurry. However, he always acknowledged that I was there by smiling as he passed me by - only to vanish in thin air!

Most of the apparitions appeared to me in human form, except for the giant. This happened one night while I was sound asleep. I was awakened to find a face that wasn't human staring right at me. There was a large bright purple glow around its body and it appeared to be over twenty feet tall. I remember how my father ran up the stairs as I lay screaming and hiding under the covers. My father tried to comfort me by convincing me that it was all just a dream.

My father thought I had a very active imagination when I told him of the events. He called them dreams, but even as a child, I knew they were not dreams. Finally, after a couple years of leaving the lights on, my visions of the beings stopped. Of course, now as a spiritually enlightened adult, I realize that these spiritual beings played a big part in my journey in life.

Family Story

My parents, Joe and Carmen, decided to make the move from Long Island, New York to Palm Beach County, Florida in 1973. My grandma Jenny, who is my father's mother, along with my brother Robert, my parents, and I all headed south to Florida.

I became an instant southern boy by moving from the big city into what, as a ten-year-old boy, I considered to be paradise. Our house was located on a lake and the fishing was good. I just loved it, especially when my parents surprised my brother and me with a rowboat.

My parents were the ideal parents. My father, a New Yorker of Italian descent, always worked hard making sure that my brother and I had the things in life that his parents (Italian immigrants from Sicily) could not afford. My dad is a very loving man and I'm very proud to have inherited those traits from him.

My mother is also always so giving. Maybe because she was the second to youngest of thirteen brothers and sisters, she had to learn how to stretch a dollar and share at a young age. My mother is from the island of Puerto Rico and moved to New York City in her early twenties to start a life in America. It's like *West Side Story* where the Italians and the Puerto Ricans got together in New York, but in my mom and dad's version, there was no dancing. But knowing my dad, there was singing!

I come from a long line of Psychics and Mediums on my mother's side, which makes me a fourth-generation psychic. My great-grandmother, Francesca, was a very well known psychic in Puerto Rico. She was a teacher of spiritualism and was known in her time to be one of the best. Her grandson, my Uncle Jose, has this gift too. When I was a child he told my mother that I had inherited the psychic gift. My mother wished that she had the gift, but it skipped her (well, at least that's what she tells me).

My father, on the other hand, is very skeptical about anything metaphysical. I'm hoping that one day he will understand why I do the work of a medium; that my purpose in life is to help people. I guess with so much negative publicity about scamming psychics, my father is afraid that people will look at me as a con artist instead of the honest person I truly am.

My last memory of having any visions of ghosts was a vision of my grandma Jenny, who lived with us for a couple of years before she passed away. She was the quintessential short Italian woman that always dressed in black and loved to cook. (I sure wish that I had learned how she cooked those Italian dishes)! I am always teasing my mother that she should have learned how to cook from Grandma Jenny, but then again my mother would have changed Grandmas' Italian recipes into Puerto Rican dishes!

After my grandmother passed, my father couldn't stand the emptiness of her bedroom so he moved me into it. I really didn't mind because it was a bigger room and it was away from all the other rooms in the house. One night as I walked into the room, I saw my Grandma Jenny sitting at the end of my bed. She smiled at me and asked how I was before she vanished into thin air. Now I realize she was telling me goodbye, because she never returned.

Life Goes On

As I got older I had a normal life. For some reason ghosts did not exist in my life as a teenager. I participated in sports and played the drums in high school, I even tried to sing in chorus. My chorus teacher used me more in playing the drums for the Chorus Jive Band than singing. I could take a hint!

On weekends I would practice with my rock band and my father made sure that I stayed out of trouble. After graduating high school, I was uncertain of what I wanted to do with my life. My father discouraged me big time on my dream of becoming a rock drummer, so I went into the family business of dry cleaning.

I married at the age of twenty-two to a woman who was much older than I was. She had three beautiful young children, Todd, Adam, and Ashley. A year later we had a baby girl together named Jessica. After the birth of Jessica, I wanted Jessica's siblings to know that I loved them as if they were my own, so I decided to adopt all of them. It was a great responsibility being a father of four children at a very young age. I believed that it was my karmic responsibility to take on this task of being a young father and to do my best to provide for my family. I'm sad to say that my marriage failed after twelve years, but having all of my kids in my life brought me much joy.

Getting Metaphysical

It so happens that it was my ex-wife who introduced me to Metaphysical Science back in1985. Metaphysical Science is the study of the Universal God Force, meaning one God for everyone, and of the supernatural; angels, spirit guides, ghosts, extraterrestrials and psychic phenomena. Traditionally, the word *metaphysics* refers to the branch of philosophy that attempts to understand the fundamental nature of all reality, whether visible or invisible.

That same year I saw a movie on television called *Out on a Limb*. It was based on a book by a famous entertainer named Shirley MacLaine who had written about her metaphysical life experiences. In her movie, Shirley experienced her soul leaving her body. First it circled her physical body where it lay on the bed; then her soul took off like a rocket right through the roof and flew over the city, bird-like on an endless flight. The soul went higher and higher until it was in deep space, far beyond the earth and moon. A long silver cord was attached to the soul, keeping it grounded to the earth. I was mesmerized, watching how the events unfolded in the movie.

After seeing this movie, I wanted to learn more. My ex-wife began to tell me of a similar experience she had when her body remained inert on the floor while her soul floated around. As she closed her eyes, she could see images. She described the experience as being quite similar to looking out of a window as she viewed different cultures of people and places.

In order for me to understand what she had seen, she drew a picture of one person she had seen during her out-of-body experience on paper. It was a bearded man who wore what looked like an old tattered sailor's cap covering his long grayish-black hair. His face was weathered and bore a scar just below his left eye, which was covered by a patch. He appeared to resemble a pirate of old. He was sitting at a table in what looked to be a library. The books on the shelves looked as old and weathered as the man. As she took a closer look at the books, she noticed that the titles of each binder had a person's name on it. The bearded man pointed to an open book on the table and asked her to read the title on the page. The book was called *My Many Lives*. As she started to read the first paragraph of the book, she felt something pull her backwards away from the book and she then floated down the hallway and out of the building to return to her physical body.

After seeing Shirley MacLaine's movie and listening to my ex-wife's story, I wanted to learn more about Metaphysical Science. Through a local Unity

Church I found out about a woman who taught Metaphysical Science. Her name was Carole Lynn Grant. I arranged to meet with her and had no idea what to expect when I got there. I thought that maybe I would see people dressed as wizards. My imagination was running wild before I arrived. Who knew, maybe there would be a woman with a crystal ball to read my future!

I entered the building and was guided to a room of approximately twenty people. I was astonished to see how normal everyone was. Carole had each person introduce themselves to the class and I soon found out many of them were working professionals and people who owned their own businesses. I really felt a little foolish about expecting to see the Wizard Merlin or Harry Potter!

Carole is not just a psychic; she is also a Channel Medium. A channel medium is like a foreign language interpreter. The medium hears the spirit, and then relays the message to the party who is interested. The knowledge and spiritual information channeled from her spirit guides was amazing.

Spirit Guides

Spirit Guides are entities that are currently in the spirit realms. These are individuals, or groups of individuals, who have agreed with a person on the earth plane to act as their guide or guardian. Usually we enter into this agreement prior to being born into a physical body with at least one *primary guide*, called the control.

It is not uncommon to have two or more guides assisting us at a given moment. Many of the guides with which we work are beings who have lived on this earth plane at one time or another (or many lifetimes), but there are guides who are from other worlds as well. Also, many of the "special guides" that come to help us with special needs or learning experiences seem to be more evolved beings, or 'old souls' who are willingly sharing their expertise and expanded knowledge with those of us still working on our path to enlightenment. (More about Spirit Guides in chapter fifteen).

During class Carole's spirit guide taught us about God's energy and how it's all around us - it's the love that we feel. The energy of love is a vibration. All of God's creation is made up of this vibration. We are all a part of God; the great "I AM." As a result, we have to look within to find God.

Carole's spirit guide also told me that I was to become a channel, a medium and a healer and that one day I would also teach of the New Age. "Wow! A medium!" I said. "You mean dead people will talk to me?" And then I wanted to know, "What is a healer?" And "Just what is this New Age stuff?"

Carole's spirit guide explained to me that a healer uses God's energy of love. This energy is channeled through the healer and, with positive thinking and love, the energy can help someone in need. I was told that the New Age is a time of awakening; of opening up to God's Energy and of believing that God is all there is. When we are lifting our vibration, we are tuning into God's energy. (More on healing in Chapter Nine and the New Age on Chapter Seventeen).

I thought to myself, "This is great! I will be able to channel spirits. When do we start?" As it turned out, we started right away. During class, Carole would have us close our eyes to bring us into meditation. She had us visualize imaginary places that we might have been or places we would want to visit. The room was so still and quiet that I felt myself drifting to sleep.

Suddenly a few women in the group yelled out loud, "Help us!" This brought the group out of meditation fast; all of our hearts were racing. "What happened?" Carole asked. There were three women from the group, a mother and her daughters, who explained that they had all witnessed a hostile Indian attack. They told the group how the band of Indians had circled their wagons and massacred everyone in the wagon train. "Wow!" Carole replied. "You all had a family past life regression together. Every one of you must have shared that experience in a past life in order for it to come out tonight."

There were other stories people told that were equally as incredible. One story was of someone leaving their body and soaring above the earth to meet with their Spirit Guides. Another story was about someone who went back in time to witness history like the wagon train bunch. Others were greeted by angels and loved ones that have crossed over.

But when it would be my turn to tell of my journey, I had nothing to say. When I closed my eyes while meditating, all I could see was black and if I looked hard enough, I could see the back of my eyelids. After a few weeks of trying, I started seeing the color purple. It was a deep purple mixed with blue. It was the color of indigo blue (this would be significant to me later). It had the shapes of floating particles like those that you would see in a lava lamp.

The Akashic Records

I asked Carole to clarify my ex-wife's out of body experience. Carole explained that my ex-wife had been invited into the halls of the Akashic Records during her out of body experience. She explained to the group what the Akashic Records are; they are a repository of information that exists in the astral realm. They hold a complete and thorough record of everything that has ever occurred, including the thoughts and feelings of every individual, all through time.

The word "Akasha" comes from Sanskrit, and means "primary substance" or "ether". These records can typically be accessed through meditation, astral journeying, or dreams. A spirit guide will assist you in entering into the hall of the Akashic Records. Once you are able to access your records, you may not need any assistance to return to them. Interestingly, how you access the records differs from person to person. They may be presented as a library of books, one single book; images on a television or movie screen, or perhaps even on a computer. How you interact with the records is a personal matter.

The Aura

Carole covered a broad range of metaphysical events and exercises in her class. That first night was about reading auras. The word aura means "atmosphere of multi-colored light" called "areola". The human aura is a multi-layered energy field that is primarily generated by the spiritual chakra energy centers within our body. The word "chakra" means wheel. Each chakra is a spinning vortex of energy that is located throughout our body. The aura reflects moods, personality traits, emotions, general well-being, spiritual abilities and evolution. It is made up of several layers, or bodies, reflecting and relating to the seven major chakras and is an important aspect of our spiritual and material life.

We practiced viewing auras. Carole had someone stand against a white wall as a bright light was reflecting off the wall. She then instructed us to look around the person's head and to shift our eyes so that the subject was slightly out of focus, which would allow us to see an aura. When it was my turn, I squinted my eyes until the person was out of focus. I felt really dumb trying to see something that was not there.

Then suddenly I could see it - I saw her aura all around her head! "I can see a small halo of yellow!" I exclaimed. "That is great! Joe saw an aura," Carole announced. I felt good until the next person tried. She didn't even have to squint her eyes; she saw it right away, stretching upwards towards the ceiling as she described the red, yellow and a lot of green colors surrounding the person's body. My ego was shot - my small halo of yellow was nothing compared to what she had seen! (More on the Aura in chapter nine).

Psychometry

The next night was psychometry night. Psychometry is the ability to read the history of certain objects by holding the object in your hand or placing it to your forehead. Usually, small personal objects such as a watch, ring, key or other personal objects are the best. Psychometry is a good way to help you with your psychic growth.

Carole had us pair off into groups and instructed everyone in the room to give a piece of jewelry to their partner. Carole had us hold the jewelry in our hand. We were to say the first thing that came into our minds. In this exercise we should be able to get in tune with the person by intuiting things like how their day went, what they had for lunch, or their favorite color.

My partner handed me her ring. I held the ring tightly in my left hand and focused my thoughts. Nothing! My mind was a blank, so I began to guess. Every guess I made was wrong. However, she was very good at this. By holding my watch, she knew about my day and what I had eaten for lunch. She even knew my favorite color. Everyone in the room was amazed at how accurate she was with everyone's reading. (More on Psychometry in Chapter Fourteen).

Harmonic Convergence

It just so happened that my early metaphysical explorations occurred just as we were approaching the advent of the Harmonic Convergence. As August 6, 1987 approached, the news media joked about this historic event. This is the time, according to prophecy of the Mayan calendar, that all of the planets in our solar system would align. This event only happens every twenty-four thousand years. This day would welcome the coming of the New Age, uniting people to pray for peace and the healing of the earth, and to raise our vibration. There was that word again that I kept running into in my journey - vibration!

I watched the sunrise that morning with my kids at the Unity Church of Palm Beach, Florida, along with several hundred other people. I don't know what I was expecting on that day. I wondered if maybe the earth was going to change, but into what? Maybe we human beings might change, but again, into what? The build-up and the anticipation of the Harmonic Convergence were driving me mad; I had so many questions but no answers. After a few hours of waiting with high expectation, I decided that it was a waste of my time and headed home.

As I watched the news that evening, reports came from all over the world that millions of people had celebrated. They celebrated in Mt. Shasta in California and at Stonehenge in Europe; they celebrated in South America, Africa and Canada. They aired people dancing at the Pyramids of Egypt and on the rooftops of New York City. All over the world, millions of people had celebrated the Harmonic Convergence.

It wasn't until a couple of years after the Harmonic Convergence that I really understood what had happened. The vibrations of the earth had changed, as evidenced when everyone in the world witnessed the Berlin wall being torn down and the fall of Communism. My journey, along with that of millions of others, had truly begun.

The Brotherhood of
Spirits

Chapter Two

It had been years since the Harmonic Convergence. I was busy being a father of four and providing for my family. I postponed my spiritual duties. Still, I had this strong desire to learn more and continue where I had left off. Years before, Carole had informed me that I would become a channel to spirits. While in pursuit of this promise, I learned of a special group that met at *The Unity in the Pines Church* in West Palm Beach, Florida with a class about how to channel your spirit guides.

Our teacher, Marilyn Raphael, is a renowned trance channel, and the author of her own book, *The Angelic Force.* A trance channel is a person who goes into a trance and a spirit entity merges with that person's body and soul. Their expressions and mannerisms will change. You can even see a physical change in their appearance.

When I first met Marilyn, I didn't know what to expect. The only other channel that I had ever met before was Carole, so I thought when you've seen one channel medium, you've seen them all. Boy, was I wrong. I mean really, really wrong! When Carole had channeled, she would hear the voice of her guide who was very knowledgeable spiritually and had the ability to express messages to everyone.

The way that Marilyn channeled her spirit guide, who went by the name Gean, was unexpected to me. I had never witnessed anything like this in my life. When Marilyn channeled, she would sit with her legs crossed and her eyes closed while meditating until she slipped into a trance. As I watched her I saw her features actually transform physically. At first I could not make out the changes very clearly. Then her facial features began to acquire a masculine look; her head became square, her brow began to protrude, and her jaw looked chiseled. After the transformation was finished, Marilyn looked like a completely different person with the characteristics of a man.

When the spirit spoke through Marilyn, the voice was deep, with a foreign accent. The entity welcomed everyone, but came across as being unfriendly. He was very arrogant and downright rude, behaving as if everyone were beneath him. I expected the entity to be wise and gentle. I thought that it should be that way because I personally think that everything of spirit should be wise and gentle, so I was greatly put off by this sarcasm towards the group.

When it was my turn to ask a question, Gean looked directly towards me and gave me a smirk as if I were wasting his time. So I came right out and asked the spirit what my purpose is in life; asking, "Why am I here?" The response from Gean was quite shocking and unexpected.

"Your purpose!" he retorted; **"Is that all you want? Your purpose, Joseph, is to take up space, to breathe the air, to breed, to aggravate others, and to invade their space! Or do you want the real reason?"**

"Yes, I want the real reason!" Then I added, "And why do you have to be so sarcastic, I thought spirits were supposed to be friendly?" I must confess, I yelled this last part out to Gean.

Unperturbed, the spirit continued to speak. **"What is Joseph's purpose? And why is he here? Well then, should we bathe Joseph in gold or silver, for he is the only privileged one in this room? This is the real purpose** as to why you are here: to remain on guard, to be a watcher, and to be a wonderful reporter. This is your purpose, for you will be proof, and always have been proof, in the past, of The Christ!"

I was dumbfounded. To remain on guard, what was that about? A wonderful reporter? 'Yeah, right!' I thought, 'I'm not a writer!' And the proof in the past to the Christ? What was going on here? I asked the spirit Gean to explain this message and he gave this response:

"You see, Joseph, you have lived many lives before; this is what is called reincarnation. You lived all of these lives in order to fulfill your karma. You have heard that 'what goes around comes around' and Joseph, each time you reincarnate, you move closer to finishing off karma. When your karma is complete, that is when your work is done on Earth; then you are welcome to reside here with your Guides. Or maybe you can choose a new life away from earth to fulfill new karma.

"Joseph, in one of your past lives, you were here on earth while Jesus visited and you witnessed his amazing miracles. You were a messenger for The Christ: a reporter, a teacher, and a scribe. Joseph, you protected him from any false rumors and threats of the nonbelievers. Now his Christ energy is with you. Joseph, once more, you will be on guard, to be a wonderful reporter and a witness to the Christ. This was your promise when you reincarnated to earth this time." Gean paused and went on to say, "Joseph is going to feel quite holy tonight!"

I was speechless! What could I say? Did I believe in this message? Maybe we should all have a big laugh! I do have to say that Gean was very sincere when it came to clarifying my purpose in life. He advised me to have trust in Marilyn's teachings and he told me that I was on the verge of becoming a noted trance channel myself.

During that summer of 1994 I attended many classes of Marilyn's to learn how to channel spirit guides. Marilyn was very patient with all of the students in her class, taking the time to explain the art of channeling and the techniques to becoming a channel.

To begin she had me sit straight up in my chair and instructed me to clear all of my thoughts; to forget the things I had to do this week and to concentrate on only what she was saying. I was to close my eyes and imagine a secluded, dimly lit room. She then had me visualize a door in the room and asked me what I saw. In my mind's eye, I saw that the room was dark, but I noticed light escaping from under the door and outlining the doorframe. The light that seemed to emanate from the door was a purplish color mixed with blue, an indigo blue. I imagined the door opening and as the rays of light passed through my body, I felt a peaceful, loving, feeling of bliss.

While I was soaking in the love from the light, my ears began to ring like the ringing in your ears on an airplane when it climbs to higher altitudes. I slipped further into a deeper trance, almost falling asleep. The ringing began to fade. Then, it finally happened. It was incredible! As I sat in my chair I felt a huge serge of energy through my body. As I went further into a trance, my arms began to rise as if they were floating in water; they were stretched in an outward position yet they still remained in place. My arms did not tire, however. Also, my chest expanded and my shoulders felt large. My breathing became heavy. Who was this entity that merged with me? The entity sat straight up in the chair, as if he were a king, and looked around proudly at everyone in the room. We (I can only describe it as "we"; the entity and I were blended as one) had no voice, just that proud physical appearance. When Marilyn asked the spirit to speak, she welcomed him and asked for a name, but there was nothing, not even a voice. It was just a physical appearance. Still, I was elated. I finally did it - I had become a trance channel!

For a long time, every time that I channeled this entity there was no voice. We were just physical and proud. Even though my body felt as though it had grown into twice my normal size, I really felt comfortable channeling this entity. Marilyn informed me that when someone channels an entity for the first time, it's like trying on a new suit or test-driving a car. The entity is learning to move the channel's limbs and to use their voice. It is getting to know the channel by sharing its vibration and merging with the body and the spirit of the channel. I felt as if the entity were a friend; I didn't mind sharing my vibrations with it. Marilyn worked with me for a few weeks as this new entity became more acquainted with me.

Even though my channeling abilities were improving, I surprised Marilyn one evening after class by quitting the group. She tried to get me to stay by telling me that I had so much potential and was doing very well. However, I was having trouble with my marriage and it was hard for me to stay focused. For the sake of my marriage, I walked away from my spiritual pursuits. I worked on fixing my marriage for over two years with failing results. Finally, we were divorced and for the first time in my life I was alone. That, and only having my kids part-time, caused me to slide into a state of depression.

My attitude had changed for the worse; I became negative about life and negative about everything. I did have friends, however. It was the generosity of my concerned friends Denise and her husband, Everett that helped me to get through this difficult time. Having been friends with me for many years, they were moved to try and cheer me up. Denise also studied metaphysics and was a spiritual healer. A spiritual healer channels the healing energy from its spiritual source to someone who needs it. The channel is usually a person whom we call a healer, and the healing energy (universal energy) is transferred to the patient through the healer's hands. The healing does not come *from* the healer, but *through* them.

Denise asked if she could balance my aura. She said it might help me feel better and less negative about everything. "Why not", I said, "What do I have to lose?" Denise had me sit in a chair and close my eyes. She began to move her hands above my head in a circular movement. "This is a way to cleanse your aura, Joe," said Denise. While she was moving her hands over my head, she kept repeating words that were uplifting and positive. Then she detected a cloud of negativity around my body that appeared like a dark haze and felt to her like a gloomy day. Denise removed the negativity while repeating words that were uplifting and positive. She repeated these words until all the negative energy had disappeared. She explained why this negative energy had bonded to me; I had not been adequately protected.

When I first opened up to channeling in Marilyn's class, I had never known about closing myself off to any negative energy or using prayers for protection. Therefore, although I channeled entities that were positive and good, I had left a void wide open and made myself vulnerable. When you are open to channeling, you must protect yourself!

As Denise continued to balance my energy, my body felt lighter and my arms started to rise. A blinding white light appeared in my mind. It was very strange because my eyes were closed, and yet I could clearly see a bright light. I started to giggle and said, "What is going on?" The giggles turned into laughs until I was laughing so hard I could not stop. It felt so wonderful. I was on a natural high. Then a voice came out of my mouth with an Irish accent. "Identify yourself!" requested Denise. "State your purpose!" There was no response, but the voice with the Irish accent kept on laughing. Denise requested again, "Identify yourself! State your purpose!" After a few more gut-wrenching laughs, the voice with the Irish lilt spoke.

"Our purpose is to create an awakening about God's energy and vibration. We are here to open the minds of the unaware."

"What is your name?" asked Denise.

After a pause, the voice stated, **"What is in a name? For we are of a collective; a collective of beings who need no names."**

Again, Denise asked, "What is your name?"

Another short pause and then the entity answered, **"If you must have a name, how about Patrick? Yes, we will call ourselves Patrick! For now, there is another to come through. Please welcome him."**

My body posture started to change, my chest flared out, and my head tilted back. This was quite familiar; I had channeled this physical entity before. I (we) sat in the chair with the air and demeanor of a king. My arms stretched out to my side with my head tilting backwards. "Identify yourself!" demanded Denise. "Who are you? What is your name?" There was nothing but silence. I came out of my trance.

That night exhausted me; however, I certainly experienced a change in my life and my attitude. My energy felt like it was over one hundred feet high! I had mixed emotions. I wanted to tell the world about what had happened, but then again, I wondered what people would think. Would they think that I was crazy? But how could I keep something this big to myself? And what would my family think? I needed to find someone to help me understand what had just happened to me and I needed to find more information on channeling.

One day I was visiting a metaphysical bookstore called *Jennie's Secret* in Lantana, Florida. While I was looking for a book on channeling, an older gentleman approached me. "It seems like you are at a lost young fellow," he said. "Are you looking for answers? My name is Whitley. Maybe I can help you find those answers." Whitley had been a channel for over thirty years with the aid of his spirit guide, Stratford. It so happened that Whitley taught many subjects on metaphysical science. He invited me to attend his weekly class.

I was thrilled to see another channel again. I had so many questions to ask about my experience. On my first night, he informed the class that tonight we would focus on channeling. This class was a beginner's group and

Whitley had not yet introduced the art of channeling to them. "Whoever in this room wants to channel, or can channel, will do this tonight," Whitley announced.

He took us into a meditation. Soon, my arms were rising up and down and I felt as if I were going to levitate out of the room. All of the sudden something happened that had never happened before - my face felt like it was being molded into a different shape. My smile became so big and bright that it felt uncomfortable. Whitley approached me and said, "Let it come through, Joe. Do not resist." In my own voice, I said, "What is happening? I can't stop smiling!" My face became so stretched with this gigantic smile that I thought I must look ridiculous to everyone. As that thought enter my mind, I started to giggle and laugh until the Irish voice came through.

"Good evening!" The entity laughed aloud. **"Laughter raises the vibrations, so everyone, let's give a big laugh!"** The entity identified himself as Patrick. **"How may we be of service to you?"**

There was stillness in the room. Then a woman from the group asked, "Joseph, why are you here? What is your purpose?" The entity gave another hearty laugh.

"Is it Joseph's purpose you wish to ask, or is it Patrick's?"

Correcting herself, the woman replied, "I meant Patrick, what is *your* purpose?"

"Patrick's purpose is to create an awakening of God's vibration and to help the people of earth to understand other dimensions of vibrations. All beings of God are made with different levels of vibrations. My purpose is to help the people of the earth plane to raise their vibrations in order to get closer to God."

After class, Whitley approached me. "Well Joe, you have a true connection. You are not making it up. You are really channeling! You are a trance channel, Joe. The difference between you and I is that I am a channel medium. I hear the voice of my guide, and forward the message to the person in need. With you, the spirit merges with your soul and expresses its personality through you. Joe, you are welcome here anytime. What I am afraid of; since this is a beginner's class, you may scare some of the students. Find a partner so you can practice. This is the only way to learn the gift God has given to you."

So the good news was that I was on my way to becoming a trance channel. The bad news was that I still needed someone to help me develop this talent. When a few weeks had passed since meeting with Whitley, it was troubling me that I had no direction as to what to do about my channeling. The thought that maybe I was even going crazy lay heavily on my mind. I was at a loss as to what I had to do with this gift.

Then one day while driving, I heard a loud "pop!" One of the tires on my Ford Explorer had blown. I pulled off the road into a parking lot and began to change the flat. When I was finished, I noticed I was parked near a store called *The Crystal Gardens*, a metaphysical bookstore! 'How ironic is this?' I asked myself.

I walked in to the store and asked the girl at the counter where I could find books on channeling. She introduced herself as Vicki and said to me, "I have just the book you are looking for and they have just arrived! The book is called *Opening Up To Channeling.* I was just unpacking the box." Talk about timing!

We chatted for a while, and she told me about her studies of the Native American Indians. She asked if I was a channel. I told her of the channeling that I experienced in Whitley's class, but that I still doubted myself. Vicki suggested that I should practice, and she volunteered to help me. "Wow, it looks like I have found my partner, without even looking," I thought.

I made arrangements to meet with Vicki at her home the following week. The date was September 28, 1996; I remember that date clearly because it was the first time I tried to channel on my own. I was accustomed to being in a group where we all had meditated and now I would be trying to do it by myself.

Mentally I went over the steps I would use to achieve this. First, I must clear my mind and use the exercise that I learned in Marilyn's class, imagining the secluded room with the door. I instructed Vicki that when my arms began to levitate and I started to giggle, Patrick would come through. The first try, nothing. I tried for what seemed to be forever, but still nothing happened. I apologized to Vicki, thinking, "Boy; she must think I am some kind of idiot". "Relax Joe", said Vicki. Just let it flow. We are in no rush. If it happens, it happens, if not, it was not meant to be at this time."

'Okay Joe,' I said to myself, 'Time to concentrate!'

Vicki put on a musical CD of Native American music. As I closed my eyes and listened to the beating of the drums and music of the flute, my arms - finally! - began to levitate. I imagined the door opening and witnessed a being that was of pure light entering into my room. When face to face with the light being, I felt the urge to giggle and laugh. Vicki then asked, "Are you with us?"

"Yes we are," said Patrick. **"We must raise our vibrations. So let's give a big laugh. How may we be of service to you?"** Patrick explained to Vicki about God's energy and his purpose of guidance and awakening. **"There will be others who will channel through Joseph. As Joseph practices, his vibrations will lift higher; the more vibrant he becomes, the more he will connect to all that there is."**

Vicki was so excited about what she witnessed that she asked me to return the very next day. As the Native American music played through her stereo, I was giggling in no time. Instead of my arms levitating, my mouth began to smile very brightly. I'd had this same feeling a few weeks ago in Whitley's class. I waited for the laughter of Patrick. Then I wondered, "Why is my face changing shape?"

Vicki asked, "Patrick, are you with us?" There was a pause. The voice wanted to come out, but it hesitated. The entity cleared my throat and began to speak. The Irish accent was gone. This entity had a gentle voice. I kept smiling real big as this being spoke.

"We are of a Collective; the Brotherhood of all things. We are Masters and Teachers of the Creator. The Collective is made up of many beings. We are of three guides who channel through Joseph." Then, in a joking manner he referred to them as 'The Three Amigos'.

OK, so I had been aware of the spirit guide Patrick who spoke with an Irish accent and who liked to joke and laugh. (I also believe Patrick was the same vision of an Irishman that had visited me as a child). But this entity was new to me. Just then, Patrick came through with laughter, explaining that the laughter raises the vibrations. He went on to explained why I was having a hard time channeling the other guides.

"Joseph, you're not accustomed to the physical changes to your body. You must relax and let the energy flow. As you become more vibrant, your vibrations will match the vibrations of the guides who seek you. In time, you will learn how to do this. It will be as easy as falling asleep."

This new entity changed the shape of my face and made my smile large, as if my face had been lifted. My hand movements were controlled, moving inwards as if they were moving the air or energy around. My hands came together to form a triangle with my fingers.

I had been reading the book, *Opening Up to Channeling by Sanaya Roman*. It helped me to open up faster to my guides. The information started coming in clearly and quickly. On our next session, the new entity announced, **"Seeing green, lots of green - isn't that the color you're projecting? I also see red, yes there is red."** Vicki then explained that she had been burning candles of those colors before she came to meet with Joe.

"Let's play a number game," said the entity. "Think of a number from one to five." Before Vicki could say ready, the entity guessed the number was two, and was correct! Then he guessed again and again was right! At one point, he was even guessing the number as she kept changing the numbers in her mind. The entity did miss when trying to guess a number using a range of one through one hundred.

"There is a lesson in this," the entity replied. **"In this game, we are showing you confirmation that this is a true channel. As vibrations are lifted, communications are shared mentally instead of physically. The higher you are in tune to a vibration, the more clearly the mind sends messages. Joseph's vibration is low; this is why communications are sometimes inaccurate. With communication interference, some messages may come out wrong. Trust your inner feeling, for that is truth. For what sounds right to you is your truth and nobody else's."**

Vicki asked the new entity if he would go by a name. **"As a child, Joseph witnessed our presence when he was awakened to the bright shimmering light. Joseph senses our energy when he meditates and channels. I appear to him in his mind as the color indigo. Joseph thought he saw nothing but purple rays of light when he meditated. He was wrong! It was me, Indigo! So the answer to your question is, yes, you may call us Indigo,"** said the entity.

Indigo is a very color- and energy-intuitive guide. I had, indeed, first had contact with him as a child. It took me over thirty years – and many steps on my spiritual path - to realize that he was there. Indigo kept teasing us about the third guide. "**He will come when the time is right. Are you curious about whom this guide is, maybe just a little? He will show himself to you, Vicki,**" said Indigo.

Suddenly, my chest flared out as I sat straight up in my chair and with a regal demeanor I looked proudly around the room. The entity folded (my) arms and took a long deep breath. I felt physical strength from this spirit. He was not new to me at all; it was the first physical entity I had channeled. Again, this entity only stayed with me for a short time. When it left my body, I deflated like a balloon, slumped back in my chair, and felt very dizzy. I did wonder who this third guide was.

Vicki mentioned my channeling to a metaphysical teacher named Glorianna who taught a psychic development class at the bookstore. She really wanted me to channel for her class. At first I told her no, because I was still insecure about my channeling. Glorianna assured me that it would be all right and that her class would be supportive.

So I attended her class. She introduced me to everyone and handed me the floor. There were about twenty people in Glorianna's class. This was the first time I was to attempt channeling for the purpose of expecting my guides to answer questions. I was extremely nervous that nothing would happen.

I positioned myself in a chair at the front of the group and had the group circle around me. I asked everyone to talk among themselves and noted that when I start to giggle, my guides would be coming in. I felt the eyes of everyone focused on me while I tried to go into a trance. While trying to go under, I could not stay focused; I kept peeking through my semi-shut eyes to see the group's reaction. "This is not going to work!" I thought to myself as I opened my eyes.

Then I had an idea. I asked Glorianna if she had something to blindfold my eyes. She handed me a silk scarf that she happened to have in her purse. I tied the blindfold over my eyes and it made a world of a difference. I felt like I was in my secluded place away from everyone. I was able to concentrate and to imagine my room where I welcomed my guides.

As my face began to change with the smile of Indigo, a woman in the room laughed. I almost stopped the connection. 'Is she laughing at me?' I wondered. 'Maybe I do look ridiculous with this big smile on my face!' I cleared my mind once more and listened for Indigo. Indigo explained to me that there would be skeptics who would disbelieve. I must learn to trust and believe in my guides because I was a nonjudgmental messenger of peace. The truth will come to those who are open. After listening to Indigo's encouraging words, I went deeper into trance. I began to giggle and the giggles turned to laughs; in his usual way, Patrick had come laughing in.

"Everyone - lets laugh! Laughter raises the vibrations! I welcome everyone here tonight, but before we start, we need a swallow of water. I would prefer a shot of Irish whiskey, but it is Joseph's body and we must respect it." I rose, as Patrick, from my chair and headed to the back of the room blindfolded. Patrick reached for a mug sitting on the counter and filled it with water. **"The throat feels a wee parched, this will do the trick!"** I took a sip without spilling a single drop. **"This is very good; it has been quite a long time since I had the sensation of water,"** said Patrick.

After a few more sips Patrick carried the mug of water back to his chair blindfolded, again not spilling a drop, and asked, **"How may we be a service to you?"**

Wow! For a minute I thought everyone had left the room, there wasn't a sound. I wished I were able to see the look on everyone's face through the blindfold. Finally, a woman from the group broke the silence by asking Patrick if she would ever find true love.

"Look what is within, for you have a shield of protection around your heart" replied Patrick. **"You have been hurt before. You must put the shield down in order to let someone love you. First you must love thyself."** Then Indigo came through; **"Yes, dear one, I am Indigo. Energy and healing is what we do. We are sending you healing energy. Pick a number from one to five. Is it two, dear one?"** She confirmed that it was. **"This is your confirmation that this is a true channel."**

The next one who spoke was the skeptic who had laughed earlier. **"How may we help you?"** asked Indigo. **"First, dear one, pick a number, one through five. The number is four."**

"That is correct! How did you know?" exclaimed the woman, amazed.

"That is your confirmation that this is a true channel. What is your question?"

The woman was an artist of designer clothing. She painted geometric objects mixed with crystals and gems on blouses. She asked Indigo whether people would feel calm and at peace with her artwork. Indigo asked her," **How do you feel when you look at your work?"**

"I feel calm and peaceful," was her reply.

"Well, there you go!" said Indigo. **"That is your answer! You knew all along!"**

"I did?" said the woman. "What do you mean?"

"You see dear one, your artwork reflects your personality and your soul. What you create in art reflects the way you feel. That feeling will come across to anyone who is open to it."

Many questions were answered that night. After the trance, I opened my eyes to see everyone in the room looking at me. "Well, how did they do?" I asked. "Amazing, they were so right!" A gentleman that was known as the "Tire King", who owned one of the biggest tire store chains in South Florida, came up afterward to thank me for the gift I had given to everyone. That night I felt really good about myself. I made sure to give credit where credit was due; God is the one that makes this possible. Every chance I get, I give thanks to God.

My channeling had improved tremendously. I loved that I was able to help people with my gift. Vicki and I met the following week and she was eager to have my guides make an appearance. She had received great feedback from Glorianna and her students and wanted to learn more about my guides.

A Message From Indigo

"Vicki, we have some information for you to share with Joseph. Picture a triangle in your mind. The top of this triangle is the new guide who is yet to come in full form. To the right is Indigo and to the left is Patrick. Now then, in the middle is Joseph. Notice the lines of the triangle connecting all of the sides together. What the line represents is the energy that flows all around the triangle, protecting Joseph from any negativity.

"This new energy is the New Age that you humans are talking about. Your vibrations are lifting higher to merge with ours. In channeling this new energy, the person who is the channel, Joseph, is now part of the Collective. Joseph's vibrations and ours are now one. Joseph is a part of the channel. He is very much aware of what is going on. He is in the light stages of channeling. Our messages are sent to him through his higher self.

On Earth, as a human, you have a physical body. Your physical body contains a spirit. This is what is called your lower self. Your higher self is a part of you; it is a part of your soul. It is located at a higher vibration. Imagine a telephone wire connecting your higher self with your lower self. This is where our channeled communication was made. We communicate to your higher self. It is then relayed to your lower self. This is how communication is possible. Your higher self knows all. It knows God's energy, and has a record of all the lives you have lived".

"The New Age is about balancing your higher self with your lower self.
As the two merge, this is where enlightenment begins.
This is when you become whole. You become Self!"

"Joseph's personality, as a channel, will change. His spirit is lifted, and he will be less stressed. At times when he talks, he will sound like the guides from the Collective. Joseph will start to be more in touch with nature and balance out. This is what the New Age is about - to lift your vibrations to ours. All new channels of this energy will become part of their guides. The old energy was different. The person who is the channel is put on hold, while spirit comes through. The old energy is not as high to them. Moreover, their awareness is not as sharp as this new energy."

Previously I had no idea as to what reporting I would be doing, it was all starting to make sense to me now. It was channeled to me that I was to be a reporter, to be on guard and proof to The Christ. That was the message I received from Marilyn's spirit guide. It was all starting to come together.

Laughter raises the Vibrations!
Patrick

The Great Spirit

Chapter Three

V icki and I wondered about this third guide who was still to come. The next time I began to channel with Vicki's help, she asked Indigo who the third guide was.

"This guide is made up of a higher vibration," replied Indigo. **"When Joseph opens up to his channeling abilities, his vibrations are lifted in stages. In the first stage, he connects with Patrick, who helps Joseph lift his vibrations. This enables him to connect with the guides who reside at a higher vibration. Joseph is now ready to raise his vibration to the next level. The new guide is ready to come through. Take care."**

As before, my body began to change. I (we) sat straight in the chair, my chest stood out proud and my arms were crossed as if I were a king. As I cleared my throat, I began to breathe heavily and without a smile, spoke in a stern, thunderous voice. This entity was not as gentle as Indigo nor as funny as Patrick, but when (we) spoke, we certainly got everyone's attention!

"Welcome. I am Sparrow Hawk! I am Law and Order of this Universe, Protector of Mother Earth, and Protector of Nature and its Creatures. I am Protector of all of God's Creations. Joseph will learn the universal language so he will communicate with all levels on earth and the universe. He will learn about nature and the earth and be a part of it.

"This is how our vibrations connect. The universe is as a circle. When facing North, the vibration is Sparrow Hawk; I am Wisdom and Spirituality! I am a part of the universe. To the East, Indigo; he is Energy, Healer, and Power! And to the West is Patrick; he is more physical, attuned to human needs and feelings. To the South is Joseph. A Rebirth; an Awakening to this new energy."

After Sparrow Hawk spoke, Patrick came through. **"Well, how was the great Sparrow Hawk? He is something else, isn't he? Well, Vicki look at the time! Its 1:30, and you said we must stop at this time."**

Vicki looked at her watch and laughed. "Yes, you're right, Patrick, it is 1:30!"

"Take care, Vicki, and God Bless." And Patrick was gone.

After all of these years of channeling the silent, regal entity (which I had begun to think of privately as "The Incredible Hulk") we finally got to hear from him! Sparrow Hawk had been the first entity to channel through me. In the past, when he had come through, (we) had no voice, only a physical appearance. "Look out, World Wrestling!" I thought, "Sparrow Hawk is in town!" When I channeled him, I felt my body expand to almost two times my size. My breathing became heavy and the power I felt was so incredible that if he were to have a physical body, he would be as big as Conan the Barbarian.

After channeling Sparrow Hawk, I told Vicki about how I became dizzy while channeling him. She suggested that I ask Sparrow Hawk to please help me, so while meditating, I did so. My body began to expand. Vicki welcomed him, and asked what lessons he had brought to teach us.

"Welcome, for I am Sparrow Hawk. Open your ears, little one, and listen to Sparrow Hawk's Purpose. Mother Earth is crying, for, like you, she lives - she is God's creation! She cries for the pollution of her lakes and rivers, the destruction of forests; her oceans, once blue and pure, are now sick!

"Sparrow Hawk's purpose is to protect Mother Earth. Humans must open their eyes! They will take care of the possessions they own, but when it is not theirs to own, they lose respect for it. Humans are invited as guests only to Mother Earth! You are the caretakers of Mother Earth and if you treat her with respect, she will return the respect you have earned. There is no other place for you to run to should the earth be destroyed. The planet earth is your home. You must treat the whole planet as you would your home."

Vicki asked what she could do to help Mother Earth. "**We need many voices to help Mother Earth. In time, we will talk about ways to save her,**" replied Sparrow Hawk.

Vicki intuited that Sparrow Hawk was an Indian Chief in another life. She asked Sparrow Hawk who he was when he lived on earth.

"**It is not who I was that is important, it is who I am! The Universe knows me as Universal Energy. I am Law and Order to the Universe. I am a part of the Universe!**

"**On Earth, I represent the Sacred Tree. The branches are all Nations. The branches grow in all directions-to the North and South, to the East and West. This connects all humans together on earth. The branches that point to the heavens will bring the Universe, the Great Spirit, and the Spiritual Brothers closer to Mother Earth.**

"**The leaves on the tree are full of life. In time they will age and die. These leaves represent humans and as the leaves age and die, so will you. The leaves will fall and fertilize the soil, which gives strength to the trees so new leaves will grow. These leaves represent the rebirth of humans.**"

Vicki asked Sparrow Hawk about the other creations of God, the animals and minerals, and whether they have Karma, and whether or not they reincarnate.

"**The hunter becomes the hunted,**" replied Sparrow Hawk. "**The wolf becomes the rabbit, the rabbit becomes the wolf. Animals experience growth by living other animal's lives. When they have fulfilled their karma in the animal kingdom and if they choose to become human, so be it! Most humans believe there is a heaven and when they die, their souls leave the earth. If you are human and can believe there is a heaven, why not believe in what Sparrow Hawk is about to tell you? This is the Soul Evolution of Mother Earth.**"

The Spirit's Life on Earth according to Sparrow Hawk

The following information is the story of a spirit's journey on Earth according to Sparrow Hawk:

Humans live in a dimension that is known as the earth plane, which is a lower vibration than all spiritual brothers who reside on a higher vibration than earth. You would know me as a sixth dimensional energy. An entity from another Universe is called a Star Child. If this entity requests to fulfill karma on the earth plane and has never lived on earth before, it must enter as a level one soul.

The First Level is Mineral. The mineral soul is of pure energy. Mother earth is billions of years old. She is alive. Her soil and minerals are filled with the souls of pure energy. The new souls to mother earth are Star Children. These souls are from other galaxies and universes, which came to the earth to learn. When they arrive, the soul is a part of Mother Earth. Like an earthworm that plows its way through the soil, this new energy will move through the earth. It is a part of all minerals on the earth.

Feel the energy in a stone; it is of pure energy. Have you ever talked to a Mountain? They do have a soul. Why not learn to talk with this lower level energy, they communicate with each other, why not with you? Those with the gifts to see Auras can see the energy of the level one soul. They will glow and twinkle. They're in tune with Mother Earth's vibration. This is how it will learn about the earth; it's a part of her. When the soul evolves, it may stay as a level one or move to the next level.

The Second Level is Vegetation. The soul of pure energy, if it chooses, becomes plant life. It will pollinate a seed until the time it is ready to surface and then there is a new world for this energy. Not quite letting go of Mother Earth with its roots planted firmly into her, the soul's new lesson is now of physical growth. The soul needs nourishment to survive; it's a physical form. It can reproduce by pollinating; the seeds are their young. The soul now will experience life and death.

The Third Level is Insects. Yes, they have a soul; those pesky little bugs! The third level for the soul is more physical. This is the first stage of having a body with organs. It will also become an aggressor. It has the knowledge to organize and colonize. It has the ability to reproduce.

The Fourth Level is Animal. Mammals, reptiles, fish and birds are part of the animal kingdom, which has a strong instinct for survival. They become the hunters and the hunted. This level has emotions; they take care of their young and of each other. This is the last level before it chooses to be human. At this point of time, most do stay in the animal kingdom and choose to become dolphins or whales instead of human, for these creatures are the most highly enlightened beings on earth.

The Fifth Level of the earth plane is Humans. Humans are the caretakers of Mother Earth. They were sent here by God to take care of her. The animals were to be protected! The environment was to be kept clean! Love and friendship were to be shared among humans; this is how God intended the earth to be.

This is the highest level of the soul in the third dimensional earth. By living as other levels, humans have the experience of Mother Earth. You have been a part of her. So quickly, you forget where you came from. The lesson for humans is about tuning into God's vibration. God created men and women in his own image. God is not a he or she. God is both. God is of both masculine and feminine energies. The human male and female represents Gods energy.

Your gender determines what energy you will receive, male or female. Due to karmic reasons, the masculine and feminine lines sometimes cross, and are directed to the wrong gender. We are all of God's children, we are the same. Remember, these things are done for that person's karma.

The Universe is made up of God's Vibration. Every living thing, and all you can see, is made up of His energy. As you can see from the level of growth you had to experience, to become human did not happen overnight. It might have taken millions of years to become what you are now. You will reincarnate until you have fulfilled all of your karma. This is when your vibration will lift into a higher place of learning.

The evolution of the human is not always what many think. Take the indigenous tribes around the world who are perceived as being primitive. These people may not have a college degree or have worshiped in a modern-day religion; however, they carry a degree in spirituality because they are in tune to God's energy. They respect the lower levels of the soul. They will take what is needed and give thanks for their sacrifice. These primitives have the knowledge of what is beyond the veil that separates the unaware from all that there is.

Sparrow Hawk Speaks on Healing Stones

Vicki had one more question for Sparrow Hawk. Her moods had been up and down recently; there was no happy medium. She wanted to know if she could use a healing stone to help her.

Sparrow hawk replied, **"Joseph, as a channel, is not educated about stones. However, I know the stone for you to use. Let us help Joseph find an answer. Name the stones you have at home."**

"OK," said Vicki. "I have tiger's eye, rose quartz, amethyst, citrine, and turquoise."

"Stop! Tell Joseph the purpose of the stone," interjected Sparrow Hawk.

Vicki replied, "Stones are used for healing and energy. Each of the stones has its own purpose. Using the right stone will help a person."

"Tell Joseph the purpose of the Citrine stone."

"Citrine stones are used to balance your Chakras. Chakra means wheel, or vortex, and is invisible to the human eye; there are seven Chakras in the human body. Each of the Chakras serves a purpose; they're used to keep our energy balanced."

Sparrow Hawk said; **"Now Vicki, what happens when your Chakras are balanced?"**

"I guess you would feel balanced," said Vicki.

"When you're in balance, you're at a 'happy 'medium, is this correct?"

"Yes, you are right!"

"Use the Citrine stone," advised Sparrow Hawk, **"for it will balance you and lift your spirits."**

"Thank you, Sparrow Hawk!"

Sparrow Hawk Tells a Story

There was an elder who lived alone in the mountains many miles from a settlement and away from his tribe, because he refused to live on a reservation. When in need of supplies, he would travel down the mountainside to the settlement.

The town's people thought the elder was crazy and senile and others would make fun of him. He was treated with prejudice and unkindness. The elder would appear to have conversations with himself, as if someone were there. At times, he would laugh out loud for no reason and when he brought his furs for trade, he would ask the imaginary person if the trades were fair.

Not everyone thought him to be crazy. So it eventually came the day that while traveling back to his home in the mountains, a fellow tribesman came to him. He treated the elder with great respect, as if he were chief. He begged the elder to return to the reservation for he was needed spiritually. The elder agreed to return. When he arrived, the people cheered and presented him with gifts. The chief of the tribe welcomed him with honors and invited him to share the fire circle.

You see, his people knew that the elder was a shaman, a spiritual leader: the one who talks to the Great Spirit. As the tribal council sat around the fire, the chief asked, what lessons have our spiritual brothers brought to us? The shaman closed his eyes and invited the spiritual brothers to join their circle to teach a lesson. They brought this lesson that I now share with you:

"We are Spiritual Brothers who reside with the Great Spirit and coexist side by side with the earth. There is a veil that separates our world from yours. The shaman has the gift to see beyond your world into other coexisting worlds. We are master and teachers of the Great Power of the Universe. Most of the people of the earth have forgotten where they came from and have forgotten about the Great Power of the universe. This is why so many are blinded to enlightenment, for they do not understand. When you are enlightened to the Great Power, you then own the Universe."

This had been a very interesting session. Sparrow Hawk had a lot to say this time. My energy felt high, as if I could go on all day. I wasn't dizzy like the first time I channeled him. I especially liked the story about the elder. The town's people thought he was a crazy Indian who talked to himself. But his own people, who were still connected to spirit, saw him as a spiritual leader, and a man with great honors. Who among us on the path to enlightenment can't relate to this?

It had been thirteen years since I was first introduced to metaphysical science. I had developed more in three months than I had in the previous thirteen years. What was next? I was anxious to find out.

It is not who I was that is important, it is who I am
Welcome I am Sparrow Hawk

Heaven Is Upon Us

Chapter Four

The morning before Halloween of 1996, I was invited to attend a séance on Halloween night hosted by none other than my channel teacher, Marilyn. It had been a couple of years since I had seen Marilyn. When I arrived she remembered me and greeted me warmly.

About sixteen people attended the séance. So that everyone would feel comfortable, she started the night out by having us play psychic games. We played "Guess the number - one to five" and "Guess what body part I'm thinking of." As the evening went on, people were feeling more relaxed with each other.

Marilyn instructed everyone to sit around the table, hold hands, and take a deep breath. She told the group that we were going to bring in spirit tonight, that it was for Halloween fun only. She instructed us that if any of us were able to channel, she asked that we not go into a trance because the séance might not work. If we were to go into a trance, it might take energy away from the spirits that would try to come through. Then Marilyn asked everyone to repeat three words to bring in spirit. Since the séance worked, I cannot print the words - if I did, there would have to be a disclaimer on this page saying "Kids, do not try this at home!"

"Notice the candle," she said. "We will make the flame dance." Then she intoned, "If spirit is in this room, let the candle flame flicker!" We all stared at the candle and waited. The anticipation in the room was very high. I could feel the hair on the back of my arms start to tingle as the candle flame began to flicker. It was bouncing back and forth!

Then she said, "Everyone concentrate. Use your mind to ask the candle to stop moving." Again, it happened - it just stopped moving! Then she announced that a spirit wanted to communicate through someone in the room. Who would it be? I felt myself slipping into a trance. I tried to hold back, since Marilyn requested that we all refrain from channeling. She approached me and asked if someone was with me. I shook my head no, reminding her that she had asked us not to go into trance.

"It's okay, Joe," said Marilyn. "Let the spirit speak." So I went into a deeper trance and the giggles came in, deepening into the laughter of Patrick.

"Good evening, I am Patrick. Let's all give a big laugh, since laughter raises the vibration. So - we are having fun and games! I see we are trying to get spirit to knock on the table. Patrick is my name. I am a guide to Joseph. There is an entity that is trying to come through. We are so sorry, for we cannot let it come through Joseph. Joseph's vibrations are in tune to ours. We cannot have him drifting in the lower levels. The spirit you have brought forth is stuck between the earth plane and the astral plane. That is where your departed will go when they feel their time on earth is not through. This is a place between heaven and earth. These souls are lost and need to be directed into the light. Enjoy your games, but sorry, for we cannot permit a being from the lower levels to come through. However, we will allow an entity whom is of a higher vibration to come through Joseph tonight."

A few minutes later, the host, Rita, had an Indian spirit come through who identified himself as being from the Shoshone tribe. As this spirit was talking through Rita, my arms began to rise and I felt the presence of energy that was unfamiliar. Marilyn pointed to me and said, "Look behind Joe's shoulder, there is a figure of a person behind him." He looked like a young man Native American. Marilyn invited the spirit to speak through me.

"**Welcome, I am known as Running Deer. We are of spiritual brothers from the Great Divine where the Great Spirit resides. Sparrow Hawk gave permission for Running Deer to speak through Joseph. We are grateful to be here, to share your circle. The Great Spirit is all there is. He is the sky and the water. The Great Spirit is our Father as the Earth is our Mother. This is how we will celebrate the full moon tonight. We would like to play the drum and sing.** "

Rita gave Running Deer a drum. He played beautiful music while chanting. He entertained the group until it was time for him to leave. Marilyn called for a break. I wondered to myself whether Running Deer was a new guide to me, or if he was just passing through.

After the break, Marilyn wanted to bring a spirit into the room. She instructed all channels to refrain from channeling. As Marilyn did her chant, I kept myself from going into trance. After about fifteen minutes, Marilyn asked for a knock. We listened. Nothing! Then, from the kitchen, we heard a creak! Was it spirit or just the settling of the building?

She asked the spirit to show itself in the hallway. We looked, but still saw nothing. When she asked the spirit to speak. It happened! We could hear a deep, muffled moan, sounding as if it were far away. It started from one side of the house and traveled to the other. As the moans got closer to where we were sitting, they grew louder. Everyone heard the moans. No one who was there could deny that something did happen that night!

While we are on the topic of messages from the spirit world, here is a message from Patrick.

Greetings, readers, it is Patrick. Have you ever wondered where you go when you die? Is there a heaven or hell? And what about ghosts, are they real? Did Frankenstein the monster defeat Dracula the vampire? Along these lines, we would like to tell you a story. You can accept this as truth or not, for you have free will. What is truth to you is your truth only.

Once there was a widowed gentleman whom we will call John. He was a very noble man and tried to do the right things in life; he would never hurt anyone. John had been widowed for twenty years or so. His wife passed on giving birth to their child Margaret, who was called Maggie. The only memory Maggie had of her mother was a portrait of her father & mother on their wedding day.

John was taken ill all of the sudden. The doctor had no hope for him. "Maggie, I am sorry," said the doctor. "Your father has taken a turn for the worse. The only thing we can do for him is to make him comfortable. It will be any day now that John will pass on. See if you can make the proper arrangements." As hours went by, John's condition worsened. Maggie did all she could to keep him comfortable. As her father lay there, he was mumbling something very faintly. Maggie listened to hear what her father was saying, but the only thing she could make out was her mother's name - Rosemary. We will listen in and see to whom John was talking.

John: How could this be? My Rose, my sweet Rose, is it really you?

Rosemary: Yes Dear John, it is I, Rosemary. I'm here to help you find peace.

John: How can it be you, Rose? It's been twenty years since I last laid eyes on you. You look so young, so beautiful, like the day we married. I have aged so much since you've been gone!

Rosemary: The day that we married was the way I chose to look in heaven. Take my hand, John, and feel the love around you.

John: Where are you taking me Rose? I'm leaving my body behind!

Rosemary: We are going into the light, John; this is where our home is. Your life on earth is over for now. It is time to come home for a rest.

John: Is this Heaven?

Rosemary: If you like to call this heaven, then, yes John, this is heaven. John, you can create anything you want here. Just give it thought and it will happen. Feel the love of all the souls here. Absorb all the knowledge and wisdom. You will learn about your growth from the life you have left behind on earth. John, your soul is alive, it will live forever. Earth is just a temporary place to grow and learn. Here is where we belong.

John: What about our Maggie? What will she do without me?

Rosemary: Maggie will be fine, John. Go to her, for she is crying. Whisper to her that she will be fine. Tell Maggie that you are home with her mother. Tell her that I love her.

John: Maggie, it is your father. Please don't cry!

Maggie: I hear your voice, but where are you?

John: I am with you, Maggie, and so is your mother.

Maggie: I don't understand; how are you with me?

John: I am in your heart, Maggie. Just listen within, and you will hear my voice. It is beautiful here. The love from everyone is unconditional. There is so much peace here. Your mother and I love you very much. Look at the portrait of us. Remember us this way because this is the way we choose to appear in heaven. Good-bye, my sweet Maggie. Your mother and I are fine. We are with God. Take care of yourself. In time we will meet again.

Heaven according to Patrick

Well now, it is Patrick. I guess we were expecting a Halloween story, something a little scary, maybe. We are so sorry - we are from the light! We come to you in love, not fear. We are unlike the Hollywood movies you are accustomed to, with Frankenstein and all other fictional monsters made for the humor, fear and enjoyment of the films. So where is the harm of a classic monster movie? The filmmakers of today have strayed from what was fictional to what is real. It is real to become negative and murder someone. These so called "horror films" portray this negative force. The hurting and killing of a person gives strength to the negative force. It may be an illusion when the film was made, but the negative message is projected, and this gives strength to all negativity in the world.

There is a negative force. Some call this the Dark Ray. Others may call it the fallen Angel, or the Devil. When you leave the earth and return to the astral plane, you will have the power to create your own reality. If you choose to create a devil in your mind, then it will be done. For this is what you have created. So remember, since in your society, people will condemn a person for their wrongdoing, if this person believes that they will go to hell, then they will. They create a living hell for themselves, because this is where they *believe* they belong. The soul will live out its experience in this lower realm until its karma is fulfilled. When time has passed, a light will appear to them along with the help of their guides. They now may pass into a higher realm, the astral realm.

Those who have taken their own life by suicide or addictions will most likely not see a heaven, but a living hell. They left the earth unhappy, escaping the reality they created on earth. When one is negative about their life on earth and their thoughts are to give up on life, they will carry this burden into the afterlife. The depression one feels will be with them in the hereafter. These souls have created a negative heaven for themselves, a hell. They will relive their life as it was on earth and experience their death over and over again, until they learn the lesson; then they will move on.

We are all God's children. God will not judge you. All He asks you to do is to believe and have trust in Him. If you have known of anyone who has committed suicide or died from an addiction, pray for God's assistance to help this person. Try to communicate with this person by thought. Help them see the light and let them know that they are loved. Let them know that God loves them and forgives what they have done to themselves. This will help them to cross over to the Astral Life of love and harmony.

Those who committed sins of murder and harm to another being will live in the lower realms for what may seem an eternity. They need to sort out the hate they have for others and learn to be one with themselves. Time of enlightenment will come for these souls after they learn their lesson.

Now, let's talk about ghosts, since this is a Halloween chapter. Who are these ghosts? Are they real? What causes the haunting, the moving of objects? You have heard the line from the *Wizard of Oz*, "Are you a good witch or bad witch?" What about ghosts, does this apply to them? Well, now, hold on to your seats, for we will explore the realms between the earth and the astral plane.

When we are departed, the soul leaves the body and has an urgency to head for the astral light. In this light, it will find its guide or family member to guide them home. If the death is a violent one, or the soul feels its time on earth is not finished, the soul will not move on. They feel they're still alive as a physical being. They are in an Etheric State. The Etheric State is a condition of the soul before it moves into an Astral State. It's a gray, misty double of the physical body. They are lost souls that can't find their way home.

If directed to the light, the soul will most likely head home. Those who run from the light are grounded to the earth. They feel the earth is where they belong. They will appear as a ghost. They will try to make their presence known, and be a part of the earth. They can move through walls, or anything physical, because they are no longer physical. If the ghost can move physical objects, it will feel it is a part of the earth. This is what might be called a Poltergeist. Stay away from the ones that cause physical pain to a person and destroy material objects. They can cause you harm.

Heaven is called the Astral Plane; also, it is known as the land of milk and honey. It is the place of learning. Heaven can be whatever you want it to be. If fishing all day is heaven to you, then that's the heaven you have created for yourself. Your thoughts are what create a heaven for you. You can be old, young or a person you were from another lifetime. It is up to you, it's the ultimate fantasy. You might think heaven is beyond the stars and the universe. It is not. Heaven is within you; it's a breath away. When you on earth whisper, we can hear you. There is no time in the Astral Plane. What may have happened a thousand years ago on earth is only minutes in this realm.

The Astral Plane is also where you review the life that you have just left and all lives you have experienced as a soul. This is where you learn from your mistakes. Heaven is where you become a creator of your own reality, as God is the Creator of all there is. That is our lesson for today. Remember that Laughter Raises the Vibration. You cannot have too much laughter in the world!

Take care and God bless you.

Patrick

The Sacred Fire Circle

Chapter Five

On the first weekend in November of 1996, I attended a Native American spiritual gathering at the Ocala National Forest in Florida. Trying to explain to my family that I was going camping with Native Americans was not easy to do. I needed to get away for some alone time because I was going through a divorce and camping out in the woods seemed like the right therapy.

I had made arrangements over the phone with a lady named Margaret Seven Feathers, who instructed me to bring a sleeping bag and camping supplies. The purpose of the trip was to get in touch with nature and learn the Native American ways. We would build a Medicine wheel and contact the tree spirits.

So here I was, driving from Palm Beach County, Florida, heading north to meet with people whom I had never met before, at a place I had never been. My guides had been bugging me to go. Of course, all along I figured that Sparrow Hawk was behind all of this since he had been wanting me to get in touch with nature. My vision was that I was really going to rough it this weekend by living off the land and learning the Native American ways. There would be no television, phones or email - just Mother Nature! I was ready for it. I even had my camping gear and sleeping bag to sleep under the stars.

When I entered the forest, I was truly blown away by the beautiful blue sky, the abundance of trees, and the wildlife. As I pulled up to the camp in my Explorer, I was surprised to see that this camp wasn't at all what I had expected. It was more like the Holiday Inn. The cabins were equipped with air conditioning, running hot water, and a cafeteria with modern appliances.

When my fellow campers arrived, I was even more surprised. "Where are the Indians?" I asked. These people were no more Native American than I was! The group belonged to the "Angelic Warrior Tribe" that met once a week at *The Crystal Garden* to learn teachings of the Native American ways. When I found Margaret Seven Feathers to ask her where my sleeping arrangements were, I saw that she, too, was not a Native American, but a New Yorker of Italian descent. I thought to myself that this ought to be interesting. She instructed me to unload my stuff at cabin eleven and advised me that we were to meet in the camp cafeteria for dinner afterwards.

Learning the Medicine Wheel

On the first night after dinner, Margaret Seven Feathers had our group of twenty-four form a circle so she could teach us the four directions of the *medicine wheel*: North, South, East, and West. The medicine wheel is an ancient and powerful symbol of the Universe. Our life travels the wheel in the same way as the earth travels around the sun, from east to west. It is a way of measuring our own progress and development and a means for assessing what we must work on next in our journey through life.

The medicine wheel is a symbolic tool that helps us to see the interconnectedness of our being within the rest of creation. The direction *East* on the wheel is where our life journey begins; it is learning to be in the here and now. The *South* is a place of summer and fullness of youth when we have physical strength and vigor for testing the physical body. The love learned in the South is the love of one person to another. The *West* is the direction of the unknown and of going within and of dreams. It is a place of testing, where the will is stretched to its utmost limit. The *North* is the place of winter; the dawning place of true wisdom. The North is seen as the direction of completion and fulfillment. There is no ending to the journey of the four directions. The human capacity to develop is infinite. The medicine wheel turns forever.

After Margaret Seven Feathers explained the workings of the medicine wheel to the group, she passed out blank name tags and asked that we each write our warrior name on the tag. Since I didn't have a warrior name, I had to think of one fast, and the only Native American name I could think of was Sparrow Hawk. I didn't think he would mind my using his name. However, I didn't want to leave out Patrick and Indigo. So I decided that what I would write on the nametag would be "The Three Amigos" to represent all three. When the group looked at me strangely and asked why I had chosen that name, I explained to them that I channeled three Spirit Guides. In order for me to include all of them, I had to decided to call them "The Three Amigos". But even as I gave that explanation, I decided that it sounded kind of dumb, so I stuck with Sparrow Hawk as my tribal name.

Prayer Ties

Next we learned to make prayer ties. Prayer ties are pieces of small 2"x2" cloth squares filled with tobacco. Each of the squares represents a prayer you can make. We were to twist the bottom of the cloth so they looked like little ghosts. With a long piece of string, we were to tie seven pieces of cloth together to make a string of ghosts. Each piece of cloth was a prayer we wished to have answered from the Great Spirit.

After everyone had finished making their ties, we headed to the lake and sat around the sacred fire circle. Most of the warriors had drums; some had rattles. At first I only watched as everyone sang and played their instruments. Margaret Seven Feathers said a special prayer before we were to burn our prayer ties. As everyone threw their prayer ties into the fire, I tossed in mine as well. We watched them burn as the warriors sang and danced around the fire, while the drums were pounding away.

Since I had played the drums in high school, I borrowed a fellow warrior's drum and joined in. As I watched the fire, the smoke began to take on a shape like a small tornado spinning up and down. All the warriors looked on, smiling at what was happening. The smoke kept spiraling for hours. I was told that our prayers were being carried to the heavens. I sat back and watched the small tornadoes of smoke rise to the heavens meditating on the Native American warriors in history.

The Vision of the Fire Circle

As the drums of my fellow warriors pounded away, I thought back to when I was a child and the vision of the Native American would appear to me. I believe that the Native American I saw then was Sparrow Hawk. I closed my eyes and imagined that I was being taken back in time to witness this spiritual gathering. As the smoke poured upwards, turning the night sky amber, and the heat from the fire became more intense, the vision of Sparrow Hawk returned to me, along with visions of his fellow warriors.

I could see Sparrow Hawk wearing a multi-colored headdress of feathers that flowed with the wind. In his hand he carried what was known as a prayer stick, which is a wooden stick wrapped with animal hides and a fox skull at the very top. Sparrow Hawk led his fellow warriors into a circle around the sacred fire. As they circled the fire, they called out the words, **"Mitakuye Oyasin,"** which means, "We are all related." The women of the tribe joined in the circle and repeated the words.

I was so taken with this vision that I found myself also chanting the words "Mitakuye Oyasin". It all seemed very real. As I danced around the sacred circle, I felt the heat of the fire and the beating of the drums shuddering through my body. Sparrow Hawk jumped up on a pile of boulders surrounding the fire, raised his right arm towards the heavens as he held the prayer stick high, and called out the word, **"Wakantanka,"** (Great Spirit) **"Please answer our prayers - Aho!"** (Amen). I opened my eyes and reflected on the vision I had just experienced. Had I just been taken back in time to witness the ceremony of the Sacred Fire Circle?

The next morning as I walked to the lake two fellow warriors, Laura and Deborah, approached me. Laura was into the Native American teachings. Deborah had come only to give Laura companionship since Laura's husband could not make the trip. The girls wanted to know more about my guides and asked me about "the Three Amigos". I informed them that Sparrow Hawk, my Native American Guide, was the one who had persuaded me to go on this trip. Indigo, on the other hand, liked to play number games and I was still learning about him. When I talked about Patrick of Ireland, Deborah informed me that she was from Ireland, too. She was here in Florida to teach a workshop. She felt compelled to ask if she could talk to Patrick, so we arranged to meet in a secluded place later in the day.

Medicine Rocks

After breakfast we gathered as a group and formed our circle. Margaret Seven Feathers had a stack of green cards, each representing the name of a medicine rock. She instructed us to pick any card from the deck, explaining that each individual would choose the right card pertaining to him or her. There are thirty-six medicine rocks in a medicine wheel and each rock would represent a piece of the medicine wheel we would build outside.

The cards made their way around the sacred circle. When it came to my turn, I pulled my card from the middle of the deck and exclaimed, "I should have known!" The card I had picked represented the stone for the direction north. It also represents Sparrow Hawk. He had made it known to me that he was the direction north on the medicine wheel and he stood for Wisdom, Spirituality, and a part of the Universe.

Now using actual rocks, Margaret Seven Feathers had us lay them in numerical order, with mine being number twelve. The rocks were to be placed in a large circle and in the middle of the circle, a row of rocks were laid facing north and south. Another row of rocks was laid facing east to west.

When we were finished laying out all thirty-six rocks, we noticed that the formation of the rocks looked like a cross in the middle of a circle. We were instructed to walk around the rocks creating a path in the grass. After picking up the rocks, the grass was left with a deep impression of the medicine wheel.

Tree Spirits

That afternoon, Margaret Seven Feathers led us into the woods to an open area for us to sit in a circle. She paired us each with a partner and began to instruct the group as to what we were to do. Our goal was to get in tune with the souls of the trees. First we were blindfolded. Our partner was to guide us so we wouldn't trip. Everyone was to find a tree and hug it so that they could feel the vibration of that tree. Margaret wanted us to listen to see if we could hear the tree speak to us. After communing with our tree and while still blindfolded, we would be led back to the circle by our partner.

My partner Stacy followed me as I walked to find my tree. The first one I bumped into was a young, small tree, so I went around it to find a larger one. I wrapped my arms around the tree and hugged it as I was told to do, sensing its vibration. My partner brought me back to the circle and took my blindfold off. It was now time to find the tree that I had hugged earlier. I started to walk in the direction of north for about twenty yards. There were about fifty trees in front of me. I had a strong urge to turn to my left and when I turned, I saw two trees standing alone. I hugged both trees and they felt very familiar to me. My partner confirmed that those were the trees I had hugged earlier. Using my intuition helped me find the trees. We were now free for about an hour to do whatever we wanted to do and were reminded that after dinner, we would meet at the fire circle.

Meeting with Patrick and Indigo

Deborah, Laura and I looked for a secluded place so I could channel Patrick. We noticed a picnic table with a bench that was under a pavilion. Laura called our attention to a sign on the wall of the pavilion calling the area "The Learning Place" and we all agreed that this was the right place. I closed my eyes and went into a meditation. Patrick came through with his usual laughter. **"Good evening! We have a fellow Irish girl with us! So how is Dublin, my dear girl?"** said Patrick.

Deborah: That is where I'm from.

Patrick: Well now, that is where Patrick is from. My last time on earth was in the eighteen hundreds before I graduated to being a guide. Are we not having a good time, my dear?

Deborah: No, Patrick, I feel out of place here. I am not into behaving like Native Americans. I wish I were back in Ireland. I really don't know why I came. Laura asked me to keep her company this weekend, so here I am.

Patrick: There is a reason and a purpose for everything, my dear child. Nothing ever happens by accident. You are supposed to be here at this place and time. You and Joseph were guided here for a purpose. Someone else would like to say hello. Take care and God Bless.

Patrick left my body and was replaced by Indigo. (Later, Deborah told me that she had noticed the shape of my face change when I channeled the Indigo energy).

Indigo: It is I, Indigo. Welcome Laura and Deborah. Patrick is correct, nothing ever happens by accident. It is unusual, isn't it? Are we correct in saying you are also a channel like Joseph?

Deborah: Yes, Indigo, you are right. I do channel.

Indigo: We know the purpose of your channeling, just as you already know your purpose of channeling. We know you must keep your information to yourself until the right person comes along. We would like you to ask your guides, when alone, if Joseph is the right person. Pick a number between one and five Deborah. The number is two.

Deborah: Yes, that is correct, Indigo.

Indigo: That is your confirmation that this is a true channel.

I returned from the state of channeling. "What was that all about?" I asked. "Are you a channel, Deborah? What was Indigo talking about?"

"I can't tell you right now, Joe," replied Deborah. "Tomorrow morning, Laura and I will channel my guides and get confirmation. Joe, I am sorry; I cannot tell you who my guides are."

"All right, I'll wait!" I replied. "And try to be patient – I'll just have to wait and see!"

But it was hard to be patient. I tried to ask Indigo about the conversation with Deborah, but he told me what I had already tried to tell myself; that I must learn to be patient and I would have to wait. I got to bed early that evening with the hope that morning would come around faster.

At sunrise I headed to the lake to wait for Laura and Deborah and while I was sitting on the dock; Laura came out of her cabin. She informed me that Deborah had channeled her spirit guides that morning. Deborah's guides had confirmed that my guides were true channels. Deborah's guides told Laura that I was on a very important mission and that it was of great importance that Deborah help me stay on the right path to fulfill my mission. I asked what mission Deborah was talking about, but Laura would only say that Deborah would inform me about my mission later, and that she would like to get together with me next week in Palm Beach. This was all she could tell me until I met with Deborah the following week.

As I loaded up my Explorer that morning and headed home, I thought back over the weekend. I had never expected something like this to happen on this trip! What was this mission that I was on? Who were Deborah's channels? Why was it so important that I meet with her? I guess I would have to wait and see!

The Secret Code

Chapter Six

I met with Deborah at Laura's home the following week. Deborah's time in Florida was limited because she had to return to Ireland in a few days. She was very excited to get started. What I learned from that meeting would forever alter my view of life and my journey. This is how our meeting went.

"Joe, for now, you must keep to yourself what I am about to tell you," said Deborah. "I know how it is when you are learning to channel for the first time, and you want to tell the world about your gift. Sorry to be the one to burst your bubble, but you must try to have more control of yourself. Channel to someone only if you are asked to, and feel comfortable with them. Many people will not understand what you are doing. You cannot take channeling lightly. It will affect you for the rest of your life. It is hard to turn back once you put both your feet in. Your life will change. Your point of view will change.

"Joe, you must have an open mind in order to accept what I am about to tell you. The material that I channel has to do with the cell structure of the Spiritual D.N.A. code. That D.N.A., the human blueprint on how God intended the human race to be, was tampered with and altered. This took place thousands of years ago. It was before the great flood that was described in the Bible.

"The earth is billions of years old. There has been life on this earth since God created it. The human race on earth was very intelligent because they were in tune with God's Vibration. The humans had the gift of visiting other coexisting worlds by using their minds or traveling by spacecraft. Other humans existed (as they do today) in higher dimensions than yours did. These humans are galactic humans. The difference between the galactic and the earth humans is that their galactic D.N.A. is the way God intended it to be. This is why they live in a higher dimension from earth. They are not to interfere with the earth's growth.

"Humans have tampered with their own Spiritual D.N.A. on earth in order to create an inferior race. The humans who did this were scientists of the lost city of Atlantis. Yes Joe, you heard me right!

The Lost City of Atlantis

"Over eleven thousand years ago, there was an island nation located in the middle of the Atlantic Ocean and that was ruled by a noble, powerful race. The people of this land had great wealth due to the natural resources found throughout their island. The island was a center for trade and commerce. The rulers of this land influenced the people of their own island as well as people in Europe and Africa.

"This was the island of Atlantis. There were many beautiful cities that were constructed of stone built throughout the land. Water flowed in through great conduits from the mountains and was distributed to the individual buildings and to the many beautiful pools. The buildings rose around the temple in the heart of the city; rising in tiers. Highly polished colored stones were used; and inlay work was prevalent.

"In the temple were enormous semi-circular columns of onyx, topaz, and beryl, inlaid with amethyst and other stones that caught the rays of the sun at various angles. Here the sacred fires burned continually with rays that are unknown today. The Atlanteans were in tune to God's Energy. As I mentioned, they had the ability to coexist in other worlds and to travel in space.

"Then the scientists of Atlantis experimented with human D.N.A. and created a new breed of humans that were inferior to the Atlanteans. The mutants were blinded to the universal energies and became somewhat primitive-minded. The Atlanteans cast off many of the mutants to other continents and a few were kept as slaves. Not all Atlanteans approved of the D.N.A. mutation and henceforth, there was havoc in the city that tore the civilization apart. When the great flood covered the earth, it destroyed the city and most Atlanteans.

"Some fled to the stars to escape the wrath of God. The mutant humans of Africa and Europe, who were unaware and uninformed, populated the new earth. There is a special code that will activate the lost memory of the human race. My guides instructed me to help you to find your code. After you have your code, the spiritual knowledge will come to you in abundance."

I had read of stories about the lost city of Atlantis, but I have never given it much thought. The way that Deborah described the island and the people that inhabited it was as if she was from there. It amazed me that she knew so much of Atlantis. Nevertheless, it was what she said next that was so hard to believe.

"Now Joe, you have had an open mind so far, so please try to stay in this frame of mind. It is time to tell you who my guides are, and who I am. You would know my guides as Extraterrestrials; I know them as the Bejianes (pronounced Ba-jee-ins) The Bejianes are a race of beings of a dimension higher than earth that are a part of The Christ Consciousness. The beings of The Christ Consciousness are made up of the Christ Energy. This energy is a very high vibration with God.

"The earth was given a man called Jesus. This man had the Christ Energy. That is why he was called The Christ. All Bejianes are a part of the same Christ Consciousness, the Christ Vibration. The Bejianes are here to help the human race of earth find their original blueprint code, to ensure them enlightenment, and for each to find their true self."

Deborah went on to describe the appearance of the Bejianes. "They physically resemble the human race, however the difference is that their eyes are large and almond shaped; somewhat like deer eyes. They have light brown skin and long jet-black hair."

She then added "In my past life, I was Bejiane; in this life, I am a Star child, meaning that I am not from your earth. I have reincarnated as a human this time around in order to fulfill the mission of an awakening for the planet earth. We are here to prepare people for the coming events. After our work is finished, and if you have trust in what I am saying, you will be on a very enlightened path. Joe, I would like to have my guides communicate with your guides. After my guides connect with the Collective, they will channel the information back to me. Is this OK with you, Joe?"

Wow, what could I say? Did I believe in what Deborah was saying - or should I run for my life? I had never thought about spirit guides as being extraterrestrial. As for the Christ Consciousness, I did have a better understanding of the meaning of The Christ. I knew that 'The Christ' is not a man; it is a very high vibration (energy) of God. This vibration was a part of the man called Jesus and this vibration is shared among other creations of God. It was all a little overwhelming, but what did I have to lose? I gave Deborah permission to communicate with my guides.

A Meeting with the Bejianes

When she connected with the Collective through the Bejianes, the Bejianes translated the messages to her. She had me lay down on the floor and asked me to close my eyes; this was a way to get in contact with my guides. As her hands hovered over my body, I felt a very intense heat pouring out of them as she informed me that she was connecting with my energy, my aura. A blanket of thick white mist appeared in my mind and I felt myself sliding into a trance as the warmth from Deborah's hands became more intense. My name, Joseph, was being called from the distance repeatedly. In my mind's eye, I tried to see through the murkiness. The voice that had called me drew near and the silhouette of an individual began to emerge from the mist. I wondered if Deborah's description of the Bejianes had influenced my thoughts or if it was possible that I could actually see them. There appeared a being that looked just like how Deborah had described the Bejianes to me. It stood as a human would stand, but it had all of the characteristics of a Bejiane with the long, straight, jet-black hair and the almond shaped eyes. It looked around seven feet tall. The clothing was made from woven cloth that appeared to be medieval. The Bejiane extended its arms and motioned me to come closer. As it began to speak to me, its voice channeled through Deborah.

"Joseph, you're only at the beginning of your journey," said the Bejiane. "You will be working as a counselor for others individually and in groups. You will heal the ones who are hurting and reunite them with the loved ones who have passed. Also, you will bring in manuscript information to teach and inform those who wish to travel the path of enlightenment along with having the gift to prophesize.

"After your work is finished with your guides, a Master Guide of the Christ Consciousness will come through. This guide will be the one to work with the people and will have healing abilities. Your Spiritual D.N.A. Code will benefit you. It will assist you in memory activation within a few weeks. You are excellent with people and your videography is excellent. You are to use your writing talents along with your videography to inform and teach. There is a lot of gold around your auric field, but mostly around the head area, meaning you are connecting with a higher power."

"Joseph, you are on the right path. Take one step at a time. You need some integration time. You are not just from this earth. You are what is called a Star Child. You have reincarnated to earth to experience the changes that are about to occur on earth. You were there during other important changes. Now you are here for the coming of the New Age.

"The earth dimension is the hardest place to live. Being unaware is such a hard task. The earth is where you will have the most growth. The Collective is all a part of the Christ Consciousness. Joseph, you are a part of the Christ Consciousness. The Christ energy is with you. This is why you are a reporter to The Christ.

"Your guide, Patrick, is a new guide like you. He is learning and he is there to help you in every way he can. He is the one to keep your spirits up and keep you grounded. Patrick is an old soul to the earth dimension. He had a lot of tough karma to go through before he graduated into a fourth dimensional being. He will help the people of the earth with their problems.

"Sparrow Hawk is not Native American like you think he is. He appears to you as a Native American because they worshipped the earth. Sparrow Hawk is Universal Energy. Like Mother Earth is alive with a soul, so is Sparrow Hawk. He has a Universal Soul. Sparrow Hawk is Law and Order of this Universe; he is a part of the Universe. He uses a great amount of energy. Try not to channel him too often until you build up your energy.

Sparrow Hawk will bring information about the earth climate changes in the future. He is earth's protector, and knows her well.

"Indigo is your main guide; he is what we call the control. He has been with you since you were born. He loves you very much. We mentioned, Joseph, that you were a Star Child. Well, Indigo is an Extraterrestrial. He is from the Quasar Atares system.

This is where you are from, Joseph. Indigo will be the one to bring you new information. Indigo is intuitive to all transformation of energy. He uses energy for healing and balance.

"Joseph, again we say, you are a Star Child. You are here for the important changes that are about to happen to the planet. Remember that you and your guides are a part of the Christ Consciousness. We are not picking up any negativity with you. We would like to give you a few protection prayers. Please use them when you are channeling. Start by using this prayer as a protection for your guides. Show them that you care and love them as much as they love you.

"Joseph, ask to be taken beyond the astral plane for teaching and guidance. Call on the Adjuster of the Light to work on your physical body. Memorize the protection prayers and use them before channeling. As a gift for you, we, the Bejianes, are giving you a technique for balancing your Chakras. Deborah has seven cards for you. We want you to study and memorize the cards. When you meet with her later, we will translate the meaning of the cards for you. God bless you, and go in peace."

Protection Prayers

Deborah gave me the protection prayers and the seven cards. She wanted me to go home to think about what had happened that day. I had certainly learned so much about the Collective and why they are with me.

I will print the protection Prayers the Bejianes gave to me:

I was to use this first prayer before any contact with my guides for protection from negativity:

I call on the Archangel Michael to fill and surround me with your blue flame of healing and protection. I ask you, dear one, to cover me,

cover me, cover me, cover me. Cover me to the front and the back, to the left and the right, above and below, and in the center. I ask you to fill and surround my auric field with your great force field of healing and protection. Nothing can enter my field on any level of being without your divine permission.

Thank you, dear one, thank you Mother-Father God. And so, it is. I now know my aura is cleared, healed and closed to all but the Christ Vibrations.

This prayer is to protect me from any harm:

I call on the Holy Spirit to shine the light of truth into all negative thought forms, all low vibrations, all race-minded thinking, all emotional trauma, and all limitations that influence my mind, my emotions, my physical body and environment adversely. Those negative thoughts and vibrations are now being filled with truth and love and dissolved by the light of divine intelligence. Thank you Mother-Father God. And so it is.

The next prayer is in case a person might give me negative thoughts or try to drain my energy. This is to be used for anyone trying to break my force field.

I call on the Holy Spirit to dissolve all psychic attacks and negative energy that I am experiencing at this time. I now release any energy, entity low vibration, astral influence, person, place, conditions, thoughts or situations into the light and love of its own being-ness. I am now released into the light and love of my own being-ness. Thank you Mother-Father God. And so it is.

I met with Deborah the following day. She asked if I memorized the protection prayer and used the Chakras balancing cards that the Bejianes gave to me. I asked her about the cards she had given me. What purpose did they serve? What country did they originate from?

Deborah gave a laugh and smiled at me, "Okay, Joe. Sit down and I will tell you," she said. "The symbols on the cards are Universal symbols that were channeled to me by the Bejianes to give to you. They hold a certain vibration to them. Beings in the universe communicate with one another by vibrations, sound and color. The symbols on the cards are vibrations. These symbols are recognized by beings that are in tune to God's vibration. The seven cards are used for balancing your Chakras. By holding your left hand over the cards, you will feel heat from them. This is the first step you must take before we can find your Spiritual D.N.A. code. Use the cards in the numerical order that they are listed."

So I used the cards that were channeled to me by Deborah. Some cards produced heat, others did not. Deborah explained to me the cards I needed would produce heat. I will print the cards with their meaning.

(1) This symbol is the vibration for the mind, the color is turquoise. This is used to dissolve all negative thoughts and to clear the mind.

(2) This vibration is for clearing the bloodstream. The color is red. Any negative energy that is absorbed into the physical body will exit the bloodstream.

(3) The vibration is green. This symbol represents the spleen. All
impurities in the bloodstream will enter the spleen to be cleansed.

(4) The vibration of this color is magenta. This is used for your psychic
sense and helps the development of intuition.

(5) The vibration is Indigo. This is for the heart, the support system of the
body. This will help it stay pure and strong.

(6) The vibration is blue. This is for health and age. This card will help
    you stay vigorous and healthy.

(7) The color is Gold. Use this card for emotions. This will help your
    moods, to relieve depression and lift you spirits.

Another Message from the Collective

Deborah informed me that the Bejianes wanted to send me another message
from the Collective. Again she had me lay on the floor as she communicated
with her guides. The word "beautiful" entered my mind while Deborah was
in her trance. I thought maybe my guides wanted me to tell her how beautiful
she was. After she came out of her trance, I told her that for some reason I was
to tell her that she was beautiful. She laughed, and told me to wait until I read
the last paragraph that she had received from the Collective. It would make
sense to me then. This is what they had to say to me:

"We know, Joseph, that it is difficult to balance all of these aspects.
A fusion is happening now of mind, body, emotion and spirit. Your vibration

must be balanced. Joseph, your mission will come. You must take more time for yourself to meditate. It is of great importance that you meditate. Ask specific questions about your next steps. Then we will show you where to go.

"**All beings are universal energies**. What is given to the third dimensional being is only a part of this energy; it is only the amount that you can handle. This is why your body is large when Sparrow Hawk comes through, for he is a universal energy. He will not harm you, Joseph. He knows how much energy your physical body can handle. The amount of energy you receive relates to the percentage of light body your physical body can handle. Joseph, you are totally capable of handling these energies. When you are given your Spiritual D.N.A. Code, your light bodies will handle an abundant amount of energy.

"**Allow your gentleness to bring harmony.** Do not allow others to upset your harmony. Remember, it is within you. This will help you on the first step of your mission. Joseph, you will be creative in your writings. Learn the art of photography for it is strength within you. Use your video talents to educate and inform. There is a new film technique for enhancement, which you are to use to bring out forms and colors. Your productions and writings will get the message across to the people. Your dreams are very important, pay attention to them. Much information will come through them.

"**Joseph, you are doing well and learning much**. You have a great eye for beauty and delivery of beauty. You are a beautiful being. You are here to embody love, peace, and non-judgment. Remember, Joseph, not one being is here to save the world. Work in conjunction to form one collective. Each being of the collective is like a piece of a puzzle. It is of great importance to work together.

"**We would like to thank the Bejianes and Deborah for being the mediums for the Collective.** This has been helpful to us to give you new messages. We used the word *beautiful* so that Deborah and Joseph will have the same confirmation about this being a true channel. Go in peace and God Bless - The Collective.**"**

Now I knew what was meant about the word *beautiful!* I asked Deborah how I would go about getting my Spiritual D.N.A. code. She told me to use the seven cards and the new symbol below that was channeled for me.

This symbol would help with energy transformation, balance and protection. Deborah informed me that the next day I was to get my code.

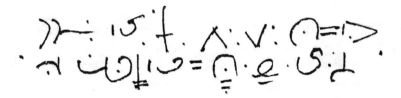

Writing is very new to me; this manuscript was written as a journal so that I wouldn't forget my experience. It was when I was writing this chapter that I realized it was the beginning of a book. I learned a great deal from Deborah. Also, I want you to know that the material channeled does not just pertain to me, the information will relate to you as well. **We are all on a journey!**

Deborah channeled my Spiritual D.N.A. Code from the Bejianes for me just as she was leaving for Ireland. I was going to miss her. She had become a good friend in the short time that I had known her.

Facing My Own Truths
and Fears

Chapter Seven

It had been over five weeks since I had received my Spiritual Genetic D.N.A. Code from the Bejianes through Deborah. For the first time in six months, I felt empty inside. Suddenly, the communication with my guides stopped and I lost my eagerness to write. There was no voice of the Collective instructing me to write.

I was worried and needed to get in touch with Deborah. I knew Laura would know where I could locate her in Ireland so I tried to call her, but her phone had been disconnected. Then I went to her home, but the house was vacant. The landlord of the property had no idea where they had gone. I was alone.

What had I done to have my guides abandon me? I went for weeks without any communication with the Collective. I had become so dependant on my guides that without their constant communication, I was going through bad withdrawals and needed a fix! The emptiness I felt inside made me feel as though I had lost a friend. What had I done, I continued to wonder, that had caused them to stop all communications with me?

Finally, after months that seemed like years, I felt the presence of my guides again. I was eager to start writing. As with everything in life, there was a reason; my guides had their purpose for that long period of quiet. Before I can explain why, I need to clarify what happened after I received my Spiritual D.N.A. Code from the Bejianes. The following is a transcript of the message I received from the Bejianes.

A Message from the Bejianes

"**Welcome Joseph, greeting from the Bejianes.** We would like to translate information to you from your guides, the Collective. We know it can be difficult at times for you, Joseph. You are learning boundaries, discernment, and the sensing of energy. Do not doubt your progress, and do not compare your progress to others, for this will block your progress. Dimensional energy is strong with you. An attempt is being made to distribute the energy equally; therefore, some fear issues may come up.

"**A Master Guide by the name of Vyamus will help you cope with all fear.** Sweating is very important, and be sure to drink plenty of water. A Master Healer by the name of Kuan Yin is administering a form of healing within you. Also, be aware an eighth century Monk of Spanish influence who will teach you to truly go within by using your gentleness and the power of prayer.

"**Joseph, practice your own form of truth.** You will receive messages that will pertain to you and this will teach you retrieval and transmission of messages. You must learn to record everything. Place all messages received in the order that makes sense to you, and then read between the lines. This is very important. Know your truth in your heart, for what is right for you. Most important is to stay focused and centered. Focus your intent on balance and do not push ahead of where you are now. Patience in this process is necessary."

Symbols in the Genetic D.N.A.

They went on to explain to me that there are ten symbols to a person's Genetic D.N.A. Code. Each symbol represents a vibration of one's true self. I was told to protect this code as though it was a secret combination to a lock;

this is the vibration code God created me with. This was for my eyes only and I was instructed not to print it in this manuscript. I will try to describe the code's details.

There are four lines to the code that are stacked as an inverted triangle. The bottom line holds one symbol and the other three lines hold three symbols on each of them. They convey a vibration and resemble the symbols I received from the Bejianes.

☐ **The bottom line** that holds one symbol represents *self*, it's my physical reality.

☐ **The second line** from the bottom represents the merging of the *higher and lower self.*

☐ **The third line** represents the search for truths and beliefs and *connection with the higher power*.

☐ **The fourth line** is the blending of the physical and the spiritual, **Ascension.** This is when one is ascended into an Ascension being.

A Message from the Collective

That was the last information that I received from Deborah's Guides, the Bejianes. The Collective had finally returned and I began to write about the changes that had occurred after receiving my Spiritual D.N.A. Code. This is what Indigo had to say:

"**Good day Joseph, we see you have felt as if we had abandoned you, and stopped our communication!** What you are experiencing may be a little confusing to you. We will try to explain this to you so you may understand what we are trying to do.

"**Joseph, when you received your code, you started going through a transition.** When in transition, you will feel as if your channeling ability has been shut down. We are still with you Joseph. The Creator who you know as God, and the Collective, are working on increasing the frequency of the vibrations you are receiving. As this transition is taking place, you may feel you are alone or out of sync with the universe. Joseph, notice the physical change to your body, the abnormal weight gains, and notice that your mind is more intuitive to people. The color blotches you are seeing are universal energy patterns that are invisible to the eyes of three dimensional beings. As you progress in your learning, the veil that separates our world from yours will be lifted. Now is the time to take care of your body, for your body is what the creator has created for you. And this body will be with you in the New Age of new times.

"Joseph, you are also dealing with karmic events. The emotions you are feeling have to do with karmic lessons. You must take care of yourself before you can help others. Your life will change and so will the people that surround you. You will attract people who are more in tune to your energies. As we progress in your teachings, you will notice that other people will begin to listen to your words as wisdom, for you will channel love and hope to humanity.

"Joseph, you are a part of the Collective. You are a representative of the third dimension here on earth. Know that when you are channeling advice for other beings, you are only offering guidance, not the solutions to their growth. You must choose what you want in life, for we cannot decide it for you. The Collective will offer advice only. When you receive the answer to what you are searching for, it is not us, the Collective, which gives you the answer. It is thee, Joseph, from whom the solution is made into form.

"Thought is what the Creator has given to human beings so that they can create their own reality as the Creator does. God has given you the power to manifest whatever you need for your spiritual growth. Many humans misunderstand the reason or the art of manifesting. When one is manifesting for personal growth, it must be done spiritually, not physically. When we refer to the word "physical", we are referring to the exposure of your human body to the earth that you walk on, the air that you breathe and the water you drink.

"God is the creator of many universes. Your universe is just one of many. The planet earth is known as the jewel of the twelfth universe. When God made the earth, it was made of beauty. There was no other planet in your galaxy as beautiful as the earth. Earth is known as the beacon in space for all souls to learn and grow spiritually. It is the schoolhouse of karmic growth, for it is the hardest place to live. When the Creator inhabited the earth with humans, he gave man free will. With this freedom, souls are to learn by having many experiences of lives for fulfillment of karma.

"Having free will gives you the choice to believe in the Creator or not. The purpose for earth is that humans can believe in God even though they cannot see him. Other creations of the creator that reside at higher vibrations are aware of all that there is. We are aware of growth. When the veil is finally lifted on earth, its beings will understand the total concept of existence. You will feel the power of the universe and all that there is.

"All physical substance of the earth is an illusion. Your body of flesh is a part of that illusion. Thought is what is real. Your spiritual self is what is real. When you leave this earth, you will shed the flesh that houses your spiritual self. You will return to a state that is of pure thought and energy. Thought is a manifestation of a higher vibration. You will find that the "real" reality is beyond the physical and in the spiritual. All events that have taken place on earth are lessons learned for your spiritual growth. Enlightenment is the grand award that is granted to thee when the lessons are learned.

"There have been many wasted lives on earth. This is why humans have reincarnated many times to this earth. The mission you have taken on earth is a task given by you to yourself before it was time to return to the earth. When living in the physical, the thought of the physical mind is not in sync with the vibrations of greater thought. This is why many lessons are not learned when you exist on the earth. When one becomes enlightened as a physical being within one's lifetime, the lessons learned are remembered when you reincarnate to earth once more. When you fulfill a lesson, you have fulfilled your karma and therefore, it is time to choose another task of spiritual growth.

"Joseph, it is time to move on with your life. The past is in the past. You must learn and grow from your experience. You must face the truths and fears that you're facing. We are at the end of an age and the beginning of the Golden Age is upon you.

It is the Age of Enlightenment. You are one of the chosen ones who volunteered to inform and teach of the Golden Age. Teach only those who will listen, for there will be many non-believers. Be the reporter you once were. Ring the bell tower and inform all that the Light of the Christ will be here!"

As Indigo had stated, I was definitely facing my own truth and fears; that pretty much summed up what I had been going through. The information I'd been getting after I received my code was strong and powerful – so much so that I was a little afraid that maybe I was going crazy.

Let's face it - the information that I was writing about was not normal stuff, and the people that I had been meeting were not normal people! How could I tell anyone that an extraterrestrial was sending me messages through a person whom I no longer knew how to find? I decided that maybe this is where the word "faith" should come in. I resolved that I would believe in myself and keep writing about all the events that were happening in my life, as directed by the Collective.

Promoter of God

Chapter Eight

When I first opened up to channeling, I was very excited about what was happening and wanted to tell the world about my gift. However, I soon realized that I wasn't the only one doing this. After meeting with Deborah and realizing how many people are channels, I was brought down off my high horse. I contacted Marilyn, my channel teacher, and she invited me to attend a group session the following week. She said this meeting was going to be a little different than the Halloween séance she had done the previous year.

When I arrived, Marilyn was passing out sheets of music for us to sing. As we were singing away she explained that this was a "way to lift the vibrations in the room."

Then she informed us that it was time for her to go into trance and her guides came through. She had two new guides channel through her since the last time I had seen her. One of them was an Irish woman who went by the name of Jenny. The other one was named James, who claimed he was the son of Joseph and the brother of Jesus.

When James came through, I was shocked to see that Marilyn's face completely changed, reflecting a square shape. Her smile became a frown and when she spoke, she sounded like a man. James had trouble speaking. In fact, the entity sounded as if it had had a stroke or a speech impediment; it was somewhat bothersome. We had to listen carefully to what James had to say because if we didn't, we would not be able to understand him. (Watching her also made me wonder if my face completely changed when I channeled Indigo).

Since this entity claimed to be the brother of Jesus, I asked him who I was when Jesus was on this earth. And his response was, *"Joseph, you were a loyal follower, and friend to my brother. You had a caring heart and did all you could to help the people understand about Jesus. You were known as Joseph of Arimathea, the secret disciple. You opened your home to him and his disciples and you were the one to give Jesus his final resting place, the tomb that he had risen from.*

You were a messenger of the Christ. Now, Joseph; you are to be a promoter of God. Your guides are the ones to help you prepare for a time when a Master will channel through you. This channel will teach those who will listen. You are to be a promoter of God! Yes, Joseph, this is your title on earth. Can you think of anything more special than that?"

Marilyn's face began to change shape again. This time she was more pleasant to look at because she looked like a woman again. The new entity smiled at me and talked with an Irish accent. This spirit had a great personality that I really loved. I began to think of her as the Dear Abby of the spirit world. She asked if she could be of help to me. I told her, "Jenny is a pretty name; my grandmother's name was Jenny." I also told her that I had recently been through a divorce and was feeling lonely. I described how hard it had been to meet someone who would understand why I channel, or even believe in what I do. I asked her what my future held.

"Well, Joe, we do hate to make predictions of the heart, but it would be hard for a spouse to understand how important your channeling is to you. Seeing a change in a person's personality and physical appearance would be hard for someone to accept. This is a great task to make-work. Only a person who is also a channel, or is familiar and understands metaphysical science could understand the work you have to do.

"There will be a promiscuous stage in your life and you will enjoy life to its fullest. You will meet new people, make new friends, and experience things you have never done before. At times, it will be like burning the candles at both ends. In the second stage of your life, you will settle down. You will meet someone who will understand you and help with your studies. You will marry once more and develop your psychic skills. The third stage is when you will be on a spiritual path. This is when you are to be a promoter of God.

"I do see a woman in your near future, Joe. She will be very close to you and love you very much. She will support your purpose and will inspire you to write, for she is a writer as well. This woman is only a breath away, for you cannot see her with your eyes, but you can feel her in your heart. This Angel that I speak of is with you and will make her presence known to you soon."

Marilyn was amazing. She was the best trance channel I had ever met. Sometimes, when you see a person channel, you wonder if they are faking it, but with Marilyn there was no question of faking. She was the one to open my eyes to channeling and to give me the message that I was to be a reporter of the Christ. And could she be right about this new woman spirit in my life?

I had more questions to ask Marilyn about my own channeling abilities, so we talked after class. I told Marilyn about meeting Deborah and her extraterrestrial friends, the Bejianes. I asked her how I could believe in something like this. People already thought I was crazy when I talked to spirits, so how would they feel if I told them the story about the Bejianes? Marilyn told me I would know what was true or not.

She asked if I felt that the information I received from Deborah was made up or true. "Of course it is true," I told her, "It's just hard to believe!"

I wanted to know how she channeled her guides the way she did. When Marilyn channeled, it looked as if her soul left her body and went somewhere while her guides completely took over. When I channel, I'm still a part of the channel. I want to stay and join in with what's going on. "Is this the right way to do this?" I asked her. She explained that when she channels, she goes into a full trance and lets the entity take over. This is why she has no recollection of what has happened or of the messages told. She explained to me that I was in the light stages of channeling; that I'm still a part of the channel. My guides may have chosen this way to communicate so I would retain all the knowledge foretold to document in the manuscript. She told me that I must learn to give more control to my guides so the messages will be clearer and free of my personal thoughts. That is why they had Deborah translate messages for me; they needed someone who was experienced enough to give me the message without any interference.

"Don't sweat it, Joe; all new channels will do this, you must learn to separate your thoughts from the thoughts of the guides," said Marilyn. I asked her how I should do this. She explained that when I am truly channeling the entities' thoughts, I would feel like I was in a trance; that is why they call it trance channeling. "When you're dreaming," she went on to explain, "You are watching the events that are taking place in your dream. You are very much aware of what is happening, and you are also a part of the dream. The difference is you are not controlling the thoughts of what you are dreaming. You have no idea what is about to happen next. It's like watching a movie for the first time.

"A trance channel works the same way as dreaming. You are aware of what is happening, but you have no idea what the thought of the entity will be until their thoughts enter your own mind. You must learn to give control to your main guide and allow only their thoughts to come through, without any interference from you. Books you have read may have given you different opinions than your guides. So naturally, you will override their thoughts with yours."

So it seemed like I must learn to give my channels full control. I recalled how I had hit a barrier when I started to channel for the first time; how I had the physical sensation of Sparrow Hawk, but no voice. It took me two years after that to channel the voice of Patrick. Marilyn is a no-nonsense person. She is determined for the person who is channeling to have a pure and true connection. There cannot be any interference with the person doing the channeling. There is an imaginary doorway that must be opened to let the true channel information come through. The hardest part for me was just letting myself go and trusting the being that is merging within me. Marilyn does believe that I am truly channeling a higher source; that I'm not acting or making the material up in my subconscious. "You just have to clean it up a bit, tune into one radio station," she told me.

What I was really afraid of was losing my mind. It was like walking on a tight rope, teetering from side to side. I could fall back, have a normal life, and forget about channeling or I could fall forward and open up to this great force of the universe.

When a person becomes a trance channel, the channel allows the spirit to completely merge with them. There is no interference from the channel; only the source can be heard, true and pure. What this means is that the entity's true personality will emerge. For instance, if the entity speaks a foreign language, then that language will be heard. The entity will have its own thoughts.

So here I was at a crossroads in my life. Channeling isn't a glamorous thing to do. Some people would think I was crazy, and some would think that I should have all the answers. The hardest part about writing this book is that I couldn't show it to anyone but those who were open to it. I could see that I would not have a normal life again, for my life had already changed. I was alone for the first time in my life. On the other hand, I was at a point in my life where I could freely take time for myself to be my own person.

A Message From Indigo

"We know it is hard for you to leave what is comfortable and familiar, Joseph. It will take a lot of discipline in order for you to open up completely to the Collective. A trust must be formed in order for you to completely let go to the Collective. Not letting go is hindering your growth and journey. When you learn to let go of the things that bring you unhappiness, then you will have the power to let yourself go to the Collective.

"We chose to have you fully aware of what is being channeled. This was done for you to learn and teach others through your writings. Always stay in the physical, Joseph, do not - I will repeat - do not put your head in the clouds and stay there. You are a physical being of the earth. You must stay grounded and live your life as a person on earth. You are not infallible. You are a being of the earth so you will have the emotions that are part of earth. Just because you are a spiritual being, doesn't make you righteous. You have temptations and emotions like every other being that resides on the earth. Remember, harmony comes from within. You are in control of your own harmony.

"When writing this book, you are to write words that the people will understand. The Collective will have separate identities in our writings. Each of us will have information that pertains to our knowledge and experience. When channeling verbally, things are going to change. The Collective will merge into one source; the vibrations of Patrick, Sparrow Hawk and I, Indigo, will be one. There is a reason for this transformation in that we are preparing you for the arrival of the Master Guide.

"In addition, this is when you will have the wisdom of the universe readily available, for this Master Guide will be a healer and teacher for all who will listen. You knew him in a past life and you will recognize his energy when you two meet again. You will channel this Master as a Collective force; meaning there will be other people in different parts of the world that will channel the same information as you. Joseph, you will work in unison with each other, teaching the words of God to all who will listen.

"Yes, this day will come and it will be your friends who will prepare you for the merging of this Great One. This emergence will not happen overnight. You cannot rush this process. You must take one step at a time and learn what the Collective will teach you. Learn to trust your inner voice and let go of your fears. We will get through this incredible journey together, for it is written by your prophets that the time of enlightenment will soon be near.

"First, you must be in physical shape. It is of great importance that your energies are at a higher vibration. Ask Sparrow Hawk for his assistance to help you get into physical shape. With proper diet and exercise, this will strengthen your aura. The aura is very important for channeling. If the aura is weak, the communication will be weak. Stay away from tobacco, alcohol, and drugs; these substances will deteriorate an aura. Stay away from bad habits such as a poor diet, the lack of exercise and fresh air.

"In meditation, yes, Joseph, during meditation, ask for Indigo's help and together we will work on your energy and Chakra alignment. It is very important that you take the time to meditate because this is the only way we can communicate. Practice your healing with universal energy. All of your intuitive strength will come from me, Indigo, When you are feeling depressed, ask for Patrick, for his energy will bring your spirits up. This is why he is with you, because he is a counselor on earthly matters. Patrick is here to make you laugh and enjoy life. Spiritual growth will come from the Collective Force. We are working to bring in God's energy and new information to you. Very soon you will receive written messages from the Christ Energy. When the time is right, a Master Guide will come through as a channel in voice and will be a part of you. When you channel this master, it will appear as if it is you; however, the difference is, the wisdom that comes forth will be one of truth.

This Master Guide will bring in God's laws
and the New Universal Commandments for the Golden Age.

The Universal Life Force

Chapter Nine

I was hired to produce a video for the ***Forever Young Institute*** in May of 1997. The ***Forever Young Institute*** is the founder of "Healthfest", which is a holistic health show featuring alternative medicine. Most of the guest speakers are physicians who practice holistic medicine and healing. While shooting the event, I ran into an old acquaintance of mine, Jane Gray Ford. I met Jane at the beginning of my metaphysical studies. She and I had both attended Carole's psychic development class in 1985. Jane is a spiritual holistic healer who practices hypnotherapy; she is also a Reiki Master.

Reiki (pronounced Ray-Kee) means the "Universal Life Force" in Japanese symbology. The word Reiki originates from the words Raku-Kei. The Raku is the vertical energy flow and the Kei is the horizontal flow of energy through the body. Reiki is universal healing energy that is transmitted through the Reiki Master to the receiver. The Reiki energy comes from the God Force; the channel giving the energy to the person in need is only the transmitter between God and the receiver. The channel is not working with their own energy at all; it is only the Creator's Life Force that comes through.

I informed Jane that I had learned that I was to become a spiritual healer according to information from Carole and Indigo. Jane invited me to attend one of her Reiki classes. The class had an attendance of about eight students; two of whom were Reiki Masters. Jane taught the class about the Aura, the Chakra system, and the art of Reiki. Here is an overview of the information she taught us about the Aura and the Chakra system.

The Aura

Everything in the Universe is a vibration. Every atom, every part of an atom, every electron, every elementary "particle", even our thoughts and consciousness are vibrations. The human aura is the energy field that surrounds the physical body. It surrounds you in all directions and is three-dimensional. In a healthy individual, it makes an elliptical, or egg shape, about the body. The ancient masters could extend their aura outward from the body for several miles. That is why they could draw such large numbers of followers in any area they traveled. The following list summarizes the meanings of various colors and shapes in the aura.

Red, Yellow and Orange:

These are warmer colors and denote extroversion, expressiveness, practicality and vitality.

Blue and Green:

These colors generally show more sensitivity and peacefulness as well as an inward and intuitive nature.

Violet and White:

These colors symbolize a vivid imagination, magic and a spiritual orientation towards life.

Also, when reading an aura, the location of the color is also important.

The **Right Side** of the body is **Masculine;** it represents the recent past, or what is leaving you.

The **Center,** above the head, indicates what you are experiencing right now.

The **Left Side** of the body is **Feminine;** it represents the near future or that which is coming into your life.

The shape of the aura will tell the mood of a person.

If the aura is **Bright and Wide**, this means you are feeling happy, outgoing, optimistic and good about life.

If the aura is **Dark and Narrow**, this could mean you are depressed, listless, afraid or ill.

If the aura is **Evenly Balanced** all around your body, this means you are balanced and consistent.

If the aura has **Gaps and Holes,** this symbolizes a loss or a will to let go of something significant.

The Chakra System

Chakra is a word which means wheel and is described as a spinning vortex of energy. The Chakras are located throughout your body. They are the primary mediators of all energy within the body and also of the energy that enters and leaves the body. The energy that is entering the body is the Universal Life Force. The Chakra system distributes energy for our mental, physical, emotional and spiritual functions. This system is made up of seven major Chakras. These Chakras are located at the points in the body where there is greater electromagnetic activity within the aura.

 The First Chakra is called the **Root or Base Chakra.** The color is red and it has a tone of the note middle C; it is the basic life force center. It is located at the base of the spine. It is also know as the Kundalini, the life force of survival. The root Chakra is tied to the circulatory system, the reproductive system, and all lower extremities. This chakra will influence activities of the testicles, ovaries, the pelvic area, legs and feet. This Chakra will open awareness of past-life talents. This is the center for life-promoting energy.

The Second Chakra is called the **Spleen Chakra,** or sexual center, which has a color of orange, and the tone of D above middle C. This is the procreative center of the body and the reproductive organ directs it. This Chakra will influence the activities of the spleen, bladder, pancreas and kidney in which it promotes the detoxification of the body. It focuses on influencing sensation and emotion and is related to the consciousness of creativity; therefore, it controls most of the personality functions.

The Third Chakra is in the **Solar Plexus;** it is the color yellow with the tone of E above middle C, located in the stomach area. It is related to the digestive center, adrenals, stomach, liver and gall bladder. It will assist the body in the assimilation of nutrients and is the link to the left hemisphere of the brain. Working from this center can ease many crippling diseases. This Chakra will open awareness to general psychic energies and experience.

The Fourth Chakra is the **Heart Chakra;** the color is green and it has the tone of F above middle C. It is tied to the heart itself and the circulatory system. It will influence the functions of the thymus gland and the entire immune system, which is linked to the right hemisphere of the brain. It is the center of higher love and healing. This Chakra is the center that awakens compassion and expression in our lives. This is the mediating center of all of the Chakras.

The Fifth Chakra is the **Throat Chakra** with a blue color and the tone of G above middle C. This Chakra is tied to the function of the throat, esophagus, mouth, teeth, thyroid and parathyroid glands and will influence the respiratory system. This Chakra will open up telepathy and consciousness to insight.

The Sixth Chakra is the **Brow, or the Third Eye,** which is the color indigo with a tone of A above middle C. This Chakra influences the function of the pituitary gland and the entire endocrine system. It is linked to the sinuses, eyes, ears and facial area in general. This is the center for clairvoyance. It is intricate in the process of the imagination and creative visualization. It can open one to spiritual vision.

The Seventh Chakra is the **Crown Chakra,** revealing the color violet with the tone of B above middle C. It is tied to the nervous system and the entire skeleton system of the body. It can open one to its higher self. This Chakra is linked to our spiritual essence and aligns us with the higher force of the universe.

The Universal Life Force according to Indigo

"The Universe is made of pure energy; it's a vibration. If you can learn to tap into this energy, you will find that the healing energy is in abundance.

Picture in your mind a river of energy, in which this river represents God's universal life force and as a channel, you must learn to bring in this loving energy and release it to the person who is in need of it. This is the art of healing. The thing is to learn how to draw on this energy and send it to the person who really needs it. Anyone can do this. First, you must have an open mind and trust, and then it will happen. The river of energy is a vibration; the human body is also a form of vibrations, everything in the Universe is a form of vibration.

"The movement of electrons and protons of every atom, every molecule, every substance, creates the vibration. God created all with this vibration. When we lift our vibrations, we are increasing the vibration frequency of the electron and protons. As the vibrations increase, they are lifted into a higher realm of existence; the more vibrant you are, the more enlightened you become. Don't think that because the Collective are made of a higher vibration, that only *we* have the gift of receiving the Universal Life Force. Anybody can do this; however, it's learning the lesson and knowing what to do with this energy. In writing this book, the Collective will only skim the surface about subjects you are learning. Once we make you aware of new things, it's up to you to go and find your teachers to help you learn these great lessons. There are teachers amongst you who are masters in their studies.

It is hard for a human to understand what an aura is because most humans cannot see one. The color of your aura will change from time to time, depending on how you feel. It is easy to know a person's personality and health when looking at their aura. There are professionals who can capture an aura image on a photograph. This is a great way to see what your aura may look like. When you have an aura picture taken, you will notice a large color glow around your body, this is your aura.

Having your aura photo is easy to do. They seat you in a chair and cover your clothing with a black cape. Then you put both of your hands on a metal plate. This may sound like the electric chair, but trust me, it isn't. With a special camera capable of what is called Kirlian photography, the photographer takes a picture that will show bands of color and light surrounding you. They will also provide you with a computer print-out explaining what the colors in your aura represent.

Technical Version

Aura photography is a visual image of how we are functioning. The technological process is complicated. The hand-shaped plates are sophisticated sensors. They measure your electromagnetic field, based on the Ayurvedic (acupressure points on the hand) system of meridians. The camera codes the energy readings into frequencies which correspond to certain colors and process the photograph, a computer sorts the information and prints the Aura Photograph. These measurements are expressed as vibration levels, which a computer chip turns into their relevant colors. A data cable from the sensor takes the information to the camera, which takes a double exposure (your image plus superimposing of colors collected from the sensors). This amazing photograph of all the collected data superimposed on the image is the Aura photo.

Joseph and I, Indigo, did an experiment with auras. Joseph had an aura photo of himself taken and his aura was the color of deep red with yellow on the left side. On a later date, Joseph had another photo taken and it was the same color, red, with yellow on the left side. We waited a few minutes and had another photo taken. Before the photographer took Joseph's picture, Joseph channeled the Indigo energy. I, Indigo, smiled for the camera and this time Joseph's aura was a deep red with yellow highlights above his head and the left side was the color of indigo."

(Note from Joseph: I had to mention to Indigo that it is great to have experiments, but he must remember that I still live on the earth plane and these experiments do cost money, therefore I said, "Next time, Indigo, take it easy on my wallet!")

Your aura can tell you a lot about yourself. Since my aura was intense red, the interpreter explained to me that I could be under a lot of stress or about to become ill. On the other hand, it could mean the opposite; that I'm burning the candle at both ends, or could even mean a strong sexual energy. In another definition, I was told the deep color of red is the color of the Christ Energy. I guess it is up to the individual to decide what definition suits them best. The left side of the aura reveals future events in your life and in my photo; mine was the color yellow, which means creativity and artistic endeavors. When I channeled Indigo, my aura turned a hint of yellow above my head, which represents spirituality and creativity. My heart was the color violet, which stands for a spiritual orientation towards life. Remember, if you have your aura image taken in the morning, the color may change by the afternoon. It's like the mood rings you find in cereal boxes that change color depending on how you feel. I've had my aura photo taken a few times within the past five years and the color has always been the same red, with yellow. I believe the red represents the Christ Energy and the yellow is the creative side that expresses itself through my writing and videography talents. My aura color changed only when I channeled Indigo.

Reiki Class

As I mentioned earlier in this chapter, Reiki is the river of energy that Indigo has told us about. The Reiki comes from the creator in which the energy is transmitted through the hands of the channel to the receptor. There are many teachers that teach the art of Reiki. You would be surprised to learn how easy it is to learn these holistic healing techniques.

Jane's class continued for several weeks. We also learned about the healing symbols used in Reiki. The symbols worked the same way as the symbols I received from the Bejianes. As I attended classes, it was almost like a refresher course to me. I felt like I had done this before because it all came so naturally; when I worked on a person, I could feel the heat surge out of my hands. This reminded me of Deborah; the way her hands produced an intense heat.

One evening, when the class was over, Jane instructed Marlene and Sharon, the Reiki Masters of our class, to give each student an attunement. An attunement is a quick effective balance of energy; it's a way of balancing your Chakras. Marlene was the one who was to give me my attunement. She put her hands on my shoulders and took a deep breath while focusing on what she was about to do. Then she put her hands on the top of my head and after a short pause, she proceeded to move her hands around my body as if she could feel the shape of my aura.

During the attunement, I felt a surge of energy entering my body. It felt similar to the energy I feel when I channel, only this time I was fully aware and not in a trance. I felt the energy with me throughout the entire healing. As I sat there, I became aware that Marlene was crying. I asked her if everything was okay.

"Oh yes," said Marlene. "You are incredible! In all of my years of healing, I have never felt such a beautiful force of energy. It is so powerful! The love that is coming through is so wonderful! I feel like I am a part of it, as it comes through you. You are a very special person, Joe, to have so much love around you. Thank you for allowing me to experience this energy with you.

I will never forget all this love." I thanked Marlene for the compliment and told her that she had described exactly what I felt when I connected with my guides. The love you feel is strong, and knowing that there is a presence beyond what we know, and that it comes from God, gives you something to hope for after your time on earth is through.

When the classes ended, Jane invited me to join with a group of women who practiced the art of Reiki. I was honored and accepted her invitation. This event took place in June of 1997 at Jane's office in Lake Worth, Florida. When I arrived, I saw that Sharon and Marlene were there, and was then introduced to six other women. Everyone took seats around a special table that had a hole in it for our faces to fit through. This was all new to me; I prepared to just sit back and watch. Jane began the class with prayer and meditation. After the meditation, she picked a person from the group to lay face down on the table and be the subject of the healing. Next Jane picked a person to perform the healing. The healer would stand at the head of the table on which the subject would lay. In this group, a pendulum was used in the healing process. A pendulum is a weight that is attached to a string so it can swing freely back and forth under the influence of the channel's spirit guide. The head person asks their spirit guide a question of healing for the person and the pendulum will swing east to west for a "yes" or north and south for a "no".

As I watched the group, I noticed that everyone held their fingers shaped into a triangle, with the index fingers positioned together to form the top of the triangle and the thumbs placed end-to-end to form the base. This is how Indigo had my fingers positioned when I channeled him. And I thought he was unique!

After the healer received a "yes" from the pendulum, everyone around the table pointed their triangular-shaped hands towards the subject on the table. It was now time to open the Chakras of the subject; this was done by what is called a "toning". Toning is a pitch, or a musical note. The group would harmonize on this note to open the person's Chakra, but moreover, to project the color of the Chakra they were opening. Each Chakra reacts to a different pitch. As I watched the group, I felt a strong presence of Indigo, so I asked Jane if it would be all right to channel Indigo for the group. Everyone in the group was okay with the idea, so I went into a channel state and Indigo came through.

"Good day, it is I, Indigo, and healing with energy is what I do. It is a pleasure to be with this group of healers. You are doing beautifully with your work in healing. Indigo would like to do healing also, if permitted."

"Yes, Indigo!" Jane answered eagerly for the group. "Of course you have our permission. We have been waiting for Joe to channel you since we met him."

I – as Indigo - walked over to the table. Indigo moved my hands over the subject's body, stopping at certain areas where he knew of injuries that a person might have had in their lifetime. As Indigo was healing, the rest of the group helped with the healing using their hands held in the triangular shape; projecting the healing energy to where it was needed. One at a time, Indigo worked on everyone in the room. Jane and Marlene were the first in the group and both noticed that the heat projected from Indigo was intense.

"It is so hot in here," said Marlene. "We have never had this much energy in the room before." Sharon, one of the healers in the group, was on the table at the moment and commented about the heat that was projecting from Indigo's hands. "It is unbelievably hot! It feels as hot as a heating pad," she said. As Indigo made his way towards her face, he asked her if there was any pain around the mouth area; she said yes, she'd had a toothache for days.

Indigo told her, **"See the color blue surrounding the tooth and releasing all pain you feel. Feel the energy of God flow through you, purifying all impurities."**

"My mouth is going numb - and the pain, I can't believe it! It's going away! Thank you Indigo, you are a keeper, you must stay in this group," cried Sharon. When Indigo was finished with the healing, Jane asked him about me.

"Will Joe be able to heal without you, or does he have to channel you, for him to heal?"

Indigo replied, **"Oh yes, Jane! Joseph will be able to heal without me, for he has done this in many lifetimes before. He is a spiritual healer and I am only his teacher. He will learn in your class and you will teach him. When the time comes for Joseph to channel a master, he will have the gift of healing. Joseph is fully aware of the events tonight and his memory of**

healing has been activated. Now he can start to heal with confidence in his abilities. Indigo would like to thank you, Jane, and everyone gathered here, for granting permission for Joseph and I, Indigo, to assist in your healing class tonight."

The following week in class, Jane asked if I could remember everything Indigo taught on healing and if I would like to start the healing class. Of course, I told her that I was. As I was getting ready to begin, a person from the group asked where my pendulum was. "You must have a pendulum. How is spirit going to give you a message?" I paused for a second to think, and then it came to me. "No, I don't need a pendulum, its natural for me, because I can heal like Indigo."

I placed my hands over the person on the table, starting to work at her shoulder area, and then worked my way to each side of her body. I felt heat in some areas and others were cool. I asked my subject if she had any problems in the shoulder area. She informed me that she had been in an auto accident a few years ago and had injured her shoulders. I kept my hands suspended over her shoulders, mentally projecting the color orange. As I was doing this, my subject commented about the intense heat she felt from my hands, and thanked me for making it feel better. As I worked on a few more people it became easier to detect the troubled areas.

It was my turn to get up on the table. Marlene was my healer, while the rest of the group projected energy towards me. As Marlene was getting a reading from her pendulum, I felt a huge surge of energy go through my body. I shouted "My shoulders!" They started to lift off the table. It was as if someone was sitting on my back, lifting my shoulder blades towards them. Marlene called out, "Look! Joe's body is moving in all directions!" Jane asked if I was okay. I told her that I was fine, but this was really weird.

I wondered what was going on now. My arms were being pulled backwards and straight up toward the ceiling. Jane explained to the class that spirit was giving me an adjustment. I really felt awkward, helpless while my body was being repositioned in all directions. But after spirit was done with me, it felt like I'd had an amazing chiropractic adjustment because I was totally energized.

Jane was impressed. This was the first time she had witnessed anything like this. "Me too," I told her, reflecting privately that since this journey had begun, a lot of strange things had happened to me!

Is Anyone Out There?

Chapter Ten

My family started to take a great interest in my channeling abilities. My mother, Carmen, always told me that I had a special gift. She had noticed that when I was a child, I spoke with my imaginary friends. We had seen psychic mediums on television that have the ability to speak to loved ones who have crossed over. We never guessed that I would be doing that myself. My mom and my youngest daughter, Jessica, helped me a lot in my channeling. They would take notes and remind me of information that I had channeled.

My cousin, Marylou, had also taken a great interest in my spiritual abilities. Marylou is the widow of my late cousin, Joey. She became very curious about what I did, especially since I had come to be the medium between her and her late husband.

One day while driving, I started thinking about my late cousin and low and behold, I found myself having a conversation with him. I thought to myself that this couldn't be happening because it wasn't normal. Was I becoming one of those types of people that talk to themselves? After speaking with Joey about my life, he thanked me for having the ability to talk to him. Then he asked if he could talk to Marylou. "Yeah, right!" I told him, "Do you want me to tell her that I am talking to her deceased husband?"

I felt that I had to have proof that I was really channeling, so I made a deal with Joey. "If you want me to tell Marylou that you are communicating with me, first you must channel information that I know nothing about so she can verify that we spoke. And if we are correct, then I will channel your messages to her." Now I found myself wanting to tell Marylou what I was doing, but I did not want to upset her.

Joey had passed away in his thirties, leaving his two boys without a dad. Marylou had loved him with all of her heart and I know that she still deeply missed him, and thought of him daily.

I didn't want to give her false hope, so I asked Joey, in my mind, to tell me a pet name he called her. After concentrating very hard, the word "cheese" came into my mind. I told Cousin Joey, "Okay, I'm going to tell Marylou that you called her cheese. Yeah, right! Let's try this again." Again, the word cheese came into my mind. So…I stopped by Marylou's home and explained to her that her husband was trying to communicate with her. When hers eyes began to tear, I got nervous and told her that he was maybe trying to talk with me. Marylou knew that I could channel, but did not yet know that I could communicate with the souls of people who have crossed over. I told her about the conversation I had with him, and how I wasn't quite sure if it was for real or just in my head. "I asked Joey what was a pet name he called you, and the only word that popped into my head was 'cheese'. Did he call you 'cheese', Marylou?" I asked. At that point, she ran into the other room crying and I thought, "Oh no, what did I do now?"

She returned with a box full of cards and romantic letters written by Joey and pointed to the top of the letters and there was the word "cheese". She told me it was personal, but Joey called her "cheese". After that night the gateway to heaven opened and allowed me to become a Medium channeling with loved ones who had crossed over.

I asked Marylou if she would accompany me to one of Jane's healing classes. Jane wanted to try something new and suggested that I go under hypnosis to see if we could look into my future. This is called Future Life Progression. Future Life Progression is the opposite of Past Life Regression. Past Life Regression is going back in time witnessing all the past lives you have lived. Future Life Progression is a trip into the future to get a glimpse of your future life events. Both are accomplished by going into a hypnotic state.

As Jane began her hypnosis on me, I felt the presence of Indigo as she began to ask me questions of the future.

Jane: Joe, in the year 1999, where are you?
Joe: I'm here in West Palm Beach.
Jane: Look around, Joe. Are the surroundings still the same?
Joe: Yes.
Jane: The year is 2001. Now where are you?
Joe: Still in Palm Beach.
Jane: Look around, Joe. What is going on in the world?
Joe: The sky is filled with fire and smoke; I see smoke all over.
Jane: We will go into 2002. Is the sky still filled with smoke?
Joe: No, the world is still the same, but there is unsettling of countries, war, and struggling over power.

My eyes were shut. I felt myself slipping into a deeper trance as Jane continued to ask her questions. In an instant, a bright, blinding flash of white light flooded my mind. After the flash, my third eye, known as the psychic eye, focused on a white bearded man sitting at a large wooden table where he was writing in some kind of tablet. The man motioned me to come forward to witness what he had written. When I approached the table, the man stood up to welcome me and that's when I recognized him. He was the weathered old man that had visited me as a child, but this time he wasn't in a hurry. He looked down and pointed to the tablet on the table that was titled <u>Never Ending Journey Of Life.</u> The vibrations of the entity were powerful as he began to speak through me to Jane.

Jane: Your voice is changing Joe. Is Indigo still with you?
Entity: *No, we are new to Joseph.*
Jane: Who are you?"
Entity: *We are not sure who we should be.*
Jane: Are you a new Guide to Joseph?
Entity: *Yes, I am.*
Jane: Describe yourself to us."
Entity: *You must go back into the ancient time before the bible was written to know who I am.*
Jane: May we call you the Ancient One?
Entity: *Yes.*
Jane: Ancient One, when will the world change?

Entity:	*The year is 2012. This is when the shift of consciousness will occur for it is happening now in your times according to prophecy."*
Jane:	Why did you pick this time to channel through Joseph?"
Entity:	*We are from the near future and this is why we are here. In time, Joseph will channel our vibration. For now, Joseph grows tired and we must stop our communication. In time he will bring our energies into your existence.*

Who was this "Ancient One"? Did he have a name? Hopefully, all these questions would be answered. Marylou told me that my posture and voice changed substantially as compared to when I channeled my other guides. When channeling the Ancient One, I have a slight curve to my back and the brow of my face protrudes out. This entity felt very tall and slim. While sitting with his legs crossed, he would bring his hand up to support his chin as he listened to Jane's questions. The voice had a soothing voice like Indigo. The only difference was that it was deeper and slightly hoarse; though neither as thunderous as Sparrow Hawk nor as overexcited as Patrick's voice.

The Rev. Fredrics

I contacted Marilyn and asked her to channel James. I thought maybe James would know who the Ancient One was, since he himself was from biblical times. This is what James had to say, *"This Ancient One is from a time before the bible was written and is also a being of light unto all other worlds. This Ancient One that you are to channel is a very powerful entity. We feel that the vibration of this entity is of the highest source, the Christ Vibration."*

Later that evening, Marilyn recommended that I go to see Rev. Ronald Fredrics, whom she believed to be an incredible channel. She told me that I would be amazed at what he could do and that he would be able to answer any question I might have about the Ancient One. He had the gift to communicate with the other side, bringing in the loved ones and other entities to answer questions we might ask. I thought that if Marilyn was impressed with this guy, then he must be good!

I made arrangements to attend an open room séance by Rev. Fredrics to be held on July 18, 1997. On the night of the séance, the room was filled with at least fifty people of all ages. There definitely were some skeptics present; I couldn't help but overhear their negative comments about the Reverend.

I figured that Rev. Fredrics would be sitting in a chair in front of the room getting ready to channel because that was how Marilyn did it. Wow, was I wrong! This gentleman was amazing. His uncanny ability to connect with spirit made me a true believer in life after death.

The evening started with Deacon Kelly passing out blank pieces of paper to all of the participants which he called billets. The pieces of paper were about 4"x 2" inches in size. We were instructed to fold them in half. On the top of the billet, we were to write the full names of three loved ones who had crossed over and their relationship to us. It had to be written in blue or black ink. In the middle of the billet and on the fold, we were to ask one question and on the bottom of the billet, we wrote our full name. Deacon Kelly warned everyone that if the billets were not filled out correctly Rev. Fredrics would not be able to answer the questions.

On my billet I wrote down the names of my cousin Joey, my Uncle Carmen (Joey's father) and my Grandmother Jenny. We were only allowed to ask one question, so I made sure it was a good one. The reason I was there that night was to get more information about the Ancient, but since we only had one question to ask, I asked if my book would be published. I finished off the billet with my full name, Joseph LoBrutto III, on the bottom, and placed it in the basket that was being passed around.

Deacon Kelly placed the basket on a podium. I waited for Rev. Fredrics to pull out a billet and read it. How else is he going to know what questions had been asked? But I was totally amazed by what he did next. He pulled out a roll of duct tape and two small pieces of cloth from his brief case. He placed the two small pieces of cloth over his eyes and proceeded to duct tape his eyes shut. He also used a scarf as a blindfold. He asked the group to sing "Amazing Grace" so that the singing could heighten the vibration in the room.

As we sang and waited for his channel source to come through, I watched him stand behind the podium and slip into a trance. I thought my eyes were playing tricks, because as Rev. Fredrics was connecting with his guide, I noticed a bluish color orb descending from above him and then entering into the top of his head. The blue orb took on the shape of Rev. Fredrics, as it became a small thin aura around his body. I asked the woman sitting next to me if she saw the blue orb around him and she looked at me as if I were crazy.

Next, the entity channeling through Rev. Fredrics, reached for the basket on the podium, pulled out a billet, placed it on the forehead of Rev. Fredrics, and asked of the audience, "**Does anyone know a Frank? The last name is like the amusement park, Coney Island.**" A person sitting behind me said, "I know a Frank Coney, he was my husband!" "**Is your name Sara?**" asked the entity. "Yes, that's me!" replied the woman. "**Frank's asked how are the boys, Pete and Danny?**" "They are fine," she replied. "**To answer your question Sara, look in the garage in the cedar chest, the papers are in there,**" said the entity through Rev. Fredics.

I was in total shock. I had never experienced anything like this before! It was as if the deceased person was in the room and you could have a conversation with them. I was amazed at what I had just witnessed, and I couldn't wait for him to read my billet. Rev. Fredrics' channel source pulled out billet after billet and with every billet he read, he provided correct answers to the questions from the loved ones brought through. He pulled out a billet from one of the skeptics in the room and asked, "**Is there a Greg in the room?**" "Yes, I am Greg." "**Well, Greg,**" said the entity, "**You did not write out this billet correctly**". After a short pause, he continued. "**You left off the names of people you want to contact. We will try to see if we can find anyone.**" There was another short pause. "**Yes, I see a woman and she tells me her name is Shirley. Is this your mother?**" *Greg acknowledged that it was.* "**She wants you to know that you should let bygones be bygones; you will know what she means,**" said the Reverend. "Yes I do, and thank you," said Greg. "Wow!" I thought, "I bet he is not skeptical anymore!"

Rev. Frederic's' channel source must have gone through over forty billets. As I anxiously awaited my turn, the anticipation was driving me crazy. At one point he crumpled a billet up and threw it on the ground. "Oh no!" I thought to myself. "Was that mine? "**This is unreadable; this billet was filled out incorrectly,**" said the Reverend. He went to the next billet. "**I see a hawk in the air.**" I thought to myself, "This has to be mine - it must be Sparrow Hawk he is talking about." But before I could say anything, he said, "**The hawk stands for the name Hawkins. Is there a Hawkins in the room?**" Someone from the front of the room said, "Yes, I'm Hawkins."

Finally he asked, "**Is there a Joseph in the room?**" "Yes! I am Joseph," I cried as I shot up from my chair. The Reverend continued, "**This is a humorous one. There is a woman dressed in black, shaking her finger at you. She is now walking over to a kettle of some sort; no, it's a pot. She is cooking, and it smells wonderful, her name is Jenny. Do you know her?**"

"Yes," I said, "She is my Grandmother!" (For the record, I had never met Rev. Ronald Fredrics in my life).

"Well, Joseph, your grandmother is an excellent cook - it smells so good in here," said the Reverend. *"She wants me to tell you to please keep up with your studies and that you are doing great. Yes, your manuscript will be published. It will sell very well and people will enjoy it! And if you think this manuscript is good, just wait until your next writing - it will be a best seller! Also, your grandmother tells me that your Uncle Carmen is here and he also says to keep on writing."*

I was in tears because my grandmother came to me just as I remembered her. When I was little and got into trouble with her, she used to shake her finger and yell at me in Italian. She was always in the kitchen cooking. She was the best! There is no doubt in my mind that this true communication happened. I knew that there was no way that Rev. Ronald Fredrics could possibly have known about my family, and certainly he could not have known the question I would ask.

After the séance I waited for Rev. Fredrics to thank him. However, he had no idea what I was talking about! He explained to me that when he channels, he is in a complete trance and has no idea about what has taken place. After hearing some of my experiences, he invited me to attend a class he taught on Friday nights. He felt I needed guidance to help me advance in my spiritual path. Wow, was I honored to be in his class. I couldn't wait for Friday to come.

When Friday did arrive, I attended Rev. Fredrics' class. I began to introduce myself to him, but he stopped me before I could tell him too much about myself. He said in this class, the students are learning psychic development and since I was new to the group and nobody knew anything about me, he wanted the group to use their intuition to learn who I was. The class reminded me a lot of Carole's class that I had attended; however, his group was much smaller, with only eight people. The reason he kept his class size small was so he was able to give one-on-one attention to his students.

The first lesson was psychometry. Rev. Fredrics passed a basket around the room that was filled with empty envelopes. We were each to put an object inside the envelope that we'd had in our possession all day. I slipped my ring off my finger and put it in the envelope. Each of the other students placed a belonging of theirs into an envelope as well.

Rev. Fredrics collected the envelopes and exchanged them among the students, making sure no one received their own. We had no idea which objects belonged to whom. To practice psychometry, we were to hold the object and focus on the first information to enter our minds. The key is not to focus too hard on the nature of the object itself and to go with the first impression of your intuition.

When I received my object, I was disappointed. I thought to myself, "How could anyone get a reading on this?" In my envelope was a small matchstick! I was afraid that I couldn't get an impression from it because it definitely wasn't personal. Deacon Kelly was the one to receive my ring. He said that the person who owned that ring was going through a transition; they were going through a big change which would result in freedom. Well, he was right, because I had just gone through a divorce and was certainly feeling free.

My turn came quickly. When I held the object, the impressions that popped in my head were of children: two boys and a girl, and the color purple. I told the class that this was new to me, but I would try my best; sharing with them the impressions I had received. The woman who owned the matchstick told me that I did great; that she does have two boys and a girl and her favorite color is purple.

Wow - maybe I was becoming a psychic! I remembered that there had been times when my mind was blank every time I tried to practice psychometry. Now I was consistently receiving images and symbols. We had fun in Rev. Fredrics class as we learned the basics in psychic development. It reminded me of what I had learned in the beginning of my journey. Then he took our psychic exploration to a new level.

First, the window blinds in the room were closed in order to have complete darkness. When the time came to shut off the lights, Rev. Fredrics brought out a silver metal object that was shaped as a cone and told us it was a trumpet. The trumpet is an instrument used by mediums to allow spirits to communicate by voice through the cone.

Rev. Fredrics placed the trumpet on the ground in front of the group and explained that spirit would move it from this spot. I couldn't wait to see this! Then Rev. Fredrics took us into meditation and everyone in the room began to chant. OOOOMMMMMMM, we intoned. He turned the lights down so low that I could no longer see my hands in front of me. The OOOOOMMMMMS were getting louder and all of the sudden there was a loud crash. Something flew and hit the wall. Then again, crash! This time it hit the wall on the opposite side of the room. The trumpet was flying all over the room and crashing into things. Then, just when I thought I had seen (and heard) it all, a voice came seemingly out of nowhere.

It had a muffled sound as if it were coming out of the trumpet. One minute I could hear the voice in front of me and than, a split second later it was behind me - then right in front again! To be honest, if I could have found the exit in the dark, I would have been out of there. As I was trying to focus on seeing the trumpet in the dark, a bright purple flash lit the entire room. I thought to myself, what was that? After the flash, the room filled with the aroma of fresh flowers. This was really spooky, like something you only see in the movies.

The voice from the trumpet began to speak; it appeared to be giving a lesson, but I was too excited about what was going on all with all of the physical manifestations to remember a single word of the lecture. After the voice stopped talking, the trumpet fell to the ground. When the lights came up, a white feather appeared from nowhere and fell in front of the group. Amazing! This night was weird, almost too weird to believe. Nevertheless, I had to ask myself why would someone go through all of that trouble to impress such a small group of people?

I have to say the Rev. Ronald Fredrics was the most amazing person I had met so far in my journey of psychic development. My cousin Marylou came to class one evening and was impressed with him as well. When I introduced Marylou to the Rev. Fredrics, he asked her why she was so sad. "There is someone in spirit who has the same name as Joseph that is in this room. Do you know him?"

"Yes," said Marylou, crying, "He is my husband." "Sit down and hold my hands," said Rev. Fredrics. "Your husband says you have cried too many tears and enough is enough. You must live your life. He will always be with you and the boys, Marylou. He is always looking out for you and wants to send you a gift. Hold on to my hands tight."

Rev. Fredrics asked Marylou to put her hands together as if she were praying. He placed his hands around her two trembling hands. Then he told her to open them. As Marylou parted her hands she saw that out of nowhere she had received a gift. It was from Joey - a blue stone that was shaped like a jellybean. "Your husband said he always gave you jellybeans, and since blue is your favorite color, he wanted to send you a blue one," said Rev. Fredrics. Marylou was crying, and I was crying for her. She asked Rev. Fredrics what was the significance of the blue circles that were formed in the stone; did they represent anything? "Yes, those are your tears, Marylou, that you no longer need to shed," he responded. Marylou said to me, "There is no way he could have put that stone in my hands. He is amazing Joe, and it's a little bit scary; but I will keep this stone for the rest of my life. Thank you, Joe, for bringing me here tonight."

For myself, I asked the Rev. Fredrics for help in channeling the Ancient One. However, he said that I must learn not to rush into the channel state. He instructed me to breathe deeply and fill my lungs with air. While breathing and with my eyes closed, I was to focus my gaze towards my nose; this is where the pineal gland is located. He informed me that this would make me feel dizzy and lightheaded, however, that would be when I would hear the voice of spirit. He called it the period of impression. I must learn to go beyond this point to be in a full trance.

Rev. Fredrics did notice a big improvement in me during a training exercise he had taught on how to read billets. He told me that he believed I had the ability to read billets. He passed out a folded piece of paper to each student. Each one had three common outdoor scenes written on it; for example, the words *boat, water* and *clouds* or *street, building* and *trees* might be on a billet. We were to hold the folded paper in our hands and use our psychic abilities in reading what was written on the billet. This is how the Rev. Fredrics learned to read billets.

Rev. Fredrics is from the old school of trance mediums and is very good at what he does. For me to be as good as him, I would need to practice what he taught me in order to fully go into a trance channel state. I had learned a great deal and my psychic ability was improving rapidly. It takes practice to learn this gift, but I guess it takes practice in anything you do to be the best. I was certainly working hard!

My Guardian Angel

Chapter Eleven

After my divorce, my daughter Jessica would make up any excuse to spend the weekends with me. Having my daughter around was the healing factor that I needed to move on with my life. Jessica has been a great help with my channeling work. I also often had my mother over on weekends to see me channel; both have been so instrumental in my spiritual growth.

One weekend I was talking to my mother about my 'new' gift of communicating with loved ones that have crossed over, and she reminded me that I had this gift years ago. She reminded me of the day my Uncle Sonny passed away in the 80's. His immediate family was in disagreement about the funeral arrangements and my father was trying to keep the peace. I was usually the quiet one in the family back then and it really wasn't any of my business, but my Uncle Sonny decided to channel through me and put his kids in their place. *To the amazement of my family members, my voice took on a pitch and timber that resembled that of my uncle and I instructed the family in how to handle the situation, which is presumably how Uncle Sonny wanted it to be handled.* My mother looked at my father and said, "Your brother is in the room." I had totally forgotten all about that day. Apparently, my cousins thought I sounded just like their father and it kind of freaked them out.

Jessica was excited about my gift to communicate with loved ones and my mother couldn't wait to get in touch with old family members. I resolved to do so, but before I was able to connect with my mother's family, I began to experience an unfamiliar vibration of energy. I asked the new presence to please show itself.

As soon as I asked, I was transported into the astral realm to a room that resembled the Sistine Chapel in Italy. The ceiling of the chapel looked like Michelangelo had painted it himself. As I was admiring the details of the painted ceiling, the roof began to retract, allowing an illumination of golden light into the room. Music began to play and an angel of great beauty descended through the open ceiling. She had chestnut brown hair and brilliant blue eyes and she radiated an aura of serenity. The angel welcomed me to share the vibration of the room. As I was in my trance encountering the new entity, Jessica and my mother noticed that my lips were changing shape and my posture actually looked like that of a woman. I began to feel 'feminine' and grew uncomfortable, so I stopped the connection with the spirit and asked for Patrick to tell me what was going on.

Patrick came in with his laughter as always. "What's the matter, Joseph? Someone wants to speak with your daughter! She is very fond of her, and why are you holding back? Yes, Joseph, she is a woman and she is beautiful! There will be a new guide to enter your life. She is the angel you were told about and she is ready to channel through you. Are you ready for her? She was once a part of your life a long, long time ago and was in love with you then, and still loves you now. Tonight when you are writing your manuscript, ask for her, for she will make her appearance known to you once more."

I reconnected again with the angel and she spoke through me to Jessica, informing her that she would do great things in her life. *"Jessica, while you are in college you will find your love and one day soon after, you will follow in your father's footsteps. You will teach, heal and do the work of mediumship."* Though I wasn't ready to channel a woman guide, I felt that Jessica needed to hear these blessed words of wisdom. Jessica was very excited to hear this and she was now even more inspired to one day go to college.

That same evening while alone in meditation, I was transported back to the astral realm to the room that looked like the Sistine Chapel and was again greeted by the beautiful angel. "Hello, Joseph. Do you remember me? I am Genevieve. It is a pleasure to connect on a spiritual level with you again! My last time physically on the earth was in the eighth century, when I lived in Normandy. This was many years ago. Of course, I know you cannot remember, Joseph.

"It is not important that I was from the eighth century; it has nothing to do with our mission. What is important are the messages given to the awakening people of the earth. In the middle ages, the time of the age was dark and the people of the earth were in a deep sleep. Now it is time to awaken the sleeping planet and educate the beautiful beings of earth about the love and harmony that God has created for us."

There was a time when the earth was new,
The trees beautiful, and the sky so blue.
Paradise was this place to be, untouched by man's impurities.
It came a time, to grow a seed, and in came humanity.
Paradise is what we had; it was a gift that didn't last.

"I do love to write poetry, Joseph. Tonight is the first time we connected in vibrations. Each time you channel my energies, we will harmonize together. It is so wonderful to finally connect with you once again, for we have so much to write about and it is now easy for you to find me."

Remember my smell of sweet perfume,
That is permeating your senses.
The feeling of love and harmony is a vibration of me.
Use your intuition and then you will see, it is I, Genevieve.

"As you know, Joseph, my name is Genevieve and I am your Guardian Angel, or in other words, I am a guide to Joseph. I do, however, prefer to be called an Angel, for that is what we were known as in the eighth century, and most beings of the earth can relate to an Angel.

"If you need a description on how we may look, you must eliminate the wings and halo. We are a non –physical being of a vibration filled with love and harmony. An aura of pure light surrounds our astral bodies. If you were to ask what our purpose is, we would tell you that it is to serve the one and only God and to deliver his love to everyone.

"We are to educate the beautiful people that are awakening on earth, so you are not alone. Our Creator is here for you and we are a part of His creations. We may not exist on the earth, but we are very much a part of it. I have lived many lifetimes; I was a part of the earth when she was young, in the beginning of her creation when humanity was seeded within her. I have lived a few lifetimes with Joseph; this is why I am his Guardian Angel. Who knows him like I do? Joseph is loved by God, the Collective, and especially by me, Genevieve. Joseph's vibration is now in sync with Genevieve, and we know he likes the feeling.

If you cannot see, you must have faith.
If you cannot hear, you must have faith.
If you cannot touch, you must have faith.
We know it's hard, to know what's true,
When one cannot feel the love come through.
Having faith is what to do, to have enlightenment
bestowed on you.

Relationships According to Genevieve

"Have you ever taken the time to study people? Have you ever noticed the difference of personalities from one person to another and how people react to each other? They can be friendly towards each other or on the other hand, the devil himself. Why do people react towards each other in different ways?

"We often ask ourselves, have we ever lived before?
And can this question really be answered?

"The purpose of not knowing that you lived past lives before is so you can have personal growth without the interference of past life events. You are to put your worries into the life you now live instead of trying to correct something you may have done hundreds of years ago in another lifetime.

"This is where Karma plays in. The word Karma means "Cause and Effect", or what goes around comes around. Suppose in another life you were a person of bad influence and the crimes you did to others were unforgivable, there was no turning to good in that life; you were just rotten to the core. The only thing that can save you is another chance, such as a new life with a different outcome. Now you are in the "Effect" part of Karma. You have left the life that was bad and have crossed over into a place of learning, but it's not the heaven you were expecting; it is a living hell because in this afterlife you are reliving all the hate you have inflicted on others.

"Then it happens; a bright light appears and a voice calls for you to enter into the light. As you travel into the light, you feel the love of beings that have forgiven you. You have learned your lesson of what is right and wrong and are ready to take the true test. It is time to pick a time to reincarnate back to Earth and face the consequence of what you did in your last life. This happens in order for you to have growth and move closer to enlightenment.

"The reason why we live life after life
So we can experience a lifetime of learning.

"People that you meet day to day may be people whom you have known in a past life. Have you ever met a person for the first time and thought that you knew them before and when you get to know them even better, it was like you had known them all of your life? You meet a person for the first time and you feel as though, 'This is it! Where have you been all of my life?' Or just the opposite can occur; you meet a person whom you dislike before even getting to know them. Maybe they did something wrong to you in a past life for you not to like them.

"The world is populated with billions of people, and of these billions of people, those that you see day to day, your family and friends, are the ones you have shared many lifetimes with. When we share a special bond with someone, most likely you have shared your life with that person in a past life. That is why you pick your parents before you are born, so as to stay in the same soul family. Your father may have been your brother or your sister may have been your mother. This is how we learn growth, when we share the experiences with the ones we love the most.

Relationships and Falling in Love.

"Why is it so hard to be with a certain person until death do us part? When we first fall in love, it's like we are in a trance and there is nothing that the other person can do to upset us because it's true love. When the fireworks of the romance are over, we will do everything in our power to find out why we shouldn't be together. Even couples that have been married for years end up in divorce. It's like the person who you knew all of your life has changed into a total stranger.

"Well, my love, this pertains to you, Joseph, and every other person who has been through this. Before you are born, you are matched up with every partner that you are involved with throughout your lifetime. There are Karmic ties involved in all of your relationships. By having free will on earth, you will have no idea of the outcome of the relationship. If your life plan became fulfilled before reincarnation, you may move on to fulfill other karma. Those who live in harmony with each other may have chosen the right path, and this couple will live their life together in harmony.

"Remember, there are still others who have karmic ties to you and if you have not met in this lifetime; perhaps you will meet in another to fulfill your karma. You do experience growth in a relationship; each person you are tied to gives you a new lesson in life and you must have this karmic lesson to grow in life. If a relationship ends, remember the lessons you have learned and try not to make the same mistakes over again in your next life. There are no right answers about finding your true love, only a lot of hard work.

Wow - Patrick was right! How can anybody not fall in love with her? It's hard to describe the vibration that I feel when Genevieve channels through me. Her vibration is different than my other guides; I get the feeling of butterflies in my stomach when I channel her. Genevieve felt comfortable channeling through me only when my daughter Jessica was in the room. I resolved to get accustomed to channeling her feminine energy. I could see that she had much to share with us.

If you look in the mirror, you will see thyself
If you look deeper, you will learn true self
Genevieve

Peace of Mind

Chapter Twelve

It had been ten years since I first channeled the Collective, and seven years since my last entry in this manuscript when I wrote this chapter. In my earlier writings, Marilyn's guide Jenny had predicted the stages that I would go through in my life. *The first was to be a promiscuous stage;* she foretold that I would enjoy life to its fullest. She told me that I would meet people and new friends and would experience things that I had never done before and that at times it would be like burning the candles at both ends. Well, Jenny was right. I put the channeling on hold and recaptured my youth. I lost weight, enjoyed life, dated a few women, and made a lot of new friends. I was burning the candle at both ends.

In the second stage of your life you will settle down, Marilyn's guide had informed me. I would meet someone who would understand me and help with my studies. I would marry once more and also develop my psychic skills. Marilyn's guide, Jenny, was right again. On August 23, 2000, I met Lisa. She is truly the woman of my dreams, and we were married in April of 2002.

The connection between us was there from the start and it was like meeting your soul mate for the first time. I never had anyone who understood me like Lisa did; she had no problem letting me be myself. The love we felt for one another is phenomenal; I have never, ever loved anyone the way I love Lisa.

Before Lisa and I got serious, I had to get the okay from one of her friends, Mary Sinatra. Mary is a cousin of the one and only Frank Sinatra. Apparently, Mary was a very intuitive person and she wanted to make sure I was right for Lisa (of course, I found this out later). It was really awesome that evening when I met with Mary and found out that she, too, was a channel. That night, her spirit guide channeled my grandmother Jenny for me. My grandmother was pleased with Lisa and told her that she was the best thing for me. And Mary just *loved* me. She said she knew I was a spiritual person before even meeting me.

After meeting with Mary, I began to feel a keen urge to channel again myself. Lisa was very supportive of my work and had helped me to connect with spirits whom had crossed over. She would assist me as people met with me in groups to hear from their loved ones who had crossed over, and hear them speak through me.

Lisa's nephew, Garrett, had crossed over in April of 2000. In one of our group sessions he came through to talk to her. He informed her that we would take a trip to California so that I could channel to both of his parents. The following summer, in July of 2001, we did, indeed, fly to California to meet Lisa's sisters, Tammy and Corene, along with their mother, Patty. My daughter Jessica and Lisa's son Steven, both fifteen years old at the time, also joined us on this trip. There was a special purpose to this trip. Earlier that June I had asked Lisa's father, Doug, for his daughter's hand in marriage. I had also asked Steven for his permission to marry his mom, and Jessica's blessing in marrying Lisa. Everyone knew I was going to pop the question on that trip.

My parents were ecstatic when they heard I was going to ask Lisa to marry me. My mom gave me her twenty five-year anniversary wedding ring to give to Lisa. My dad gave me his wedding ring, telling me that it had brought him and my mother over forty years of happiness and may it also bring forty and more years of happiness to Lisa and me.=

My soon to be brother-in law, Bobby, had rented a houseboat on Lake Shasta. This is where I would spend a few days to get to know the new in-laws. The lake was beautiful, surrounded by trees and many mountains. From a distance we could see Mt. Shasta, which is known for being a very spiritual place. It reminded me of the place I had envisioned as a child, the place where Sparrow Hawk had taken me. The energy was so strong there that I felt I needed to channel. But how could I do this? Here it was, the first time I was meeting Lisa's family, and I didn't want to freak them out. But the voice of Garrett filled my head and pleaded with me to communicate with his parents.

A few days passed, and I got to know the family a little bit better, but I was still nervous about asking Lisa to marry me. My nerves were so bad that I crashed the houseboat into the ski boat they rented! My soon to be sister-in-law, Tammy, was yelling, "Abandon ship! Every man for him self! We're going to sink!" Well, the good thing was that the ski boat didn't sink, but the bad thing was that I had put a good size hole in the boat. What a hell of a way to make a first impression!

Later that day, while Lisa went ashore, I apologized to her sisters for smashing the boat. I told them what was weighing heavily on my mind; that I was going to ask their sister to marry me. They both gave me big hugs, and were welcoming me into the family, when Lisa returned to the boat. "What's going on?" Lisa asked. The sisters covered up by saying, "Joe was so upset about almost sinking us! We were just consoling him to make him feel better." After everybody knew what my intentions were, my nerves settled down.

The last night on the boat, Tammy mentioned to me that she had learned from Lisa that I was a Medium, and that Garrett had spoken to her through me. "Since the death of our son," Tammy said, "We have explored our options by going to well known mediums to see if Garrett would give them a message. There are so many people at these gatherings that we get lost in the crowd and have no chance for receiving any messages. I wound up leaving there heart-broken, knowing my son wants to communicate, but that he cannot get through. Are you able to do this for us, Joe?" At this point, my heart was in my throat. I felt such sorrow for her; I could never imagine losing a child! "I can try, but please don't get upset if he does not come through," I told Tammy. "I've been out of practice, and I don't want to give you any false hope. I know that you and Bobby are familiar with channeling, but your mother and Patty and Corene are not. Even your daughter, Gwendolyn, and

Lisa's son, Steven, haven't seen me channel. Only Lisa and Jessica have seen what I can do. I will try, but you need to advise your family as to what I'm about to do." Tammy and Lisa explained to the family about the concept of channeling. Lisa went on by saying, "I really don't want you to think what Joe does is strange because it might not be what you are expecting. So please have an open mind tonight and have faith in Joe's ability to connect with Garrett." Jessica told them about the Collective, who they were and how they made their presence known as they came through. "My dad gets a little nervous when he does this with new people, so have a little patience, until he connects with his guides," she urged them.

When I channel with a group, I blindfold my eyes so there are no distractions. I asked everyone to talk among themselves for a bit while I went into meditation. I warned them that If I started to laugh, that would mean that Patrick was connecting with me. "The guides will ask if you have any questions, or they might answer questions before they are asked. So bear with me, as I go into a trance."

I went into my trance and immediately, I felt the presence of Patrick. My giggles began and Patrick made his entrance. "Greetings! Laughter raises the vibrations!" he proclaimed. Patrick explained that he was there to open the minds of the unaware. He stood up blindfolded and entered the boat's galley to fill a mug with water. "The throat feels a little parched, a wee sip of some water will do the trick," said Patrick in his lilting Irish brogue. Lisa's son, Steven was astonished! "I can't believe how Patrick knows exactly where he is walking. He's roaming around the boat and helping himself to a drink while blindfolded!" exclaimed Steven.

After Patrick had everyone's attention, he announced that Indigo would make his appearance. A big smile appeared across my face and Indigo came through. "Good day to you. It is I, Indigo. Why do we have sad faces when someone who loves you would want you to be happy? A few would like to say hello. A man and a woman would like to be heard. This man has thick-rimmed glasses and has the letter H in his name and the woman goes by the name of Fran. Also, I see a golden nugget. "I know them!" said Tammy. "It's Harold and Fran. They were like parents to me growing up. I lived with them for a while when I moved to California. And as to the golden nugget, well that is our golden retriever named Nugget that is with my Garrett."

Indigo explained, **"Fran and Harold send you and Bobby their love and bid you not to worry; that they are taking care of your son."**

"Garrett is here with us and is loved very much," said Fran.

Now I channeled Garrett words. *"Yes, Mom and Dad, I'm fine. Look, Nugget is with me!"* said Garrett. *"I'm sorry for what I have put you both through. Please forgive my friend for being careless while driving. I'm loved here and have peace. Please do not worry about me, and live your life happily. I know how much you miss me, and I can feel the pain and sorrow you carry everyday. It saddens me to know that I cannot take the pain away. I remember when I was a young child and my goldfish died. I was grieving heavily over my fish when you and dad comforted me by telling me that my goldfish will be in heaven living in a big pond. Well, Mom and Dad, I'm here with God and family living in my big pond. I just wanted you to know that I will always be near. "I'm still a part of your lives; I'm just in another place and I'm always looking over your shoulders, Mom! Dad, please take care of my car; we worked hard on it. Gwen, it's yours if you want it. Life is really short and I want you to please live your lives to the fullest. I love you all and I promise we will see each other again and relive all of the memories we shared together."*

"That is all for tonight," said Indigo. "Sparrow Hawk will now share a gift with you. Go outside and visit the wildlife that surrounds your boat. Tammy, Bobby and Gwen, every owl that makes its presence known to you is a gift from Garrett to show his love for you." "Thanks for giving a hoot!" Garrett added.

We all went topside to witness the amazing sight of many deer surrounding our boat. In the distance we heard the sound of a hooting owl. That evening was truly an inspirational moment.

After our stay on Lake Shasta, I took the family out to lunch at a steak house in Napa. This would be the day I would ask Lisa to marry me. It was July 6, 2001, my 38th birthday. After the meal I stood up to thank the family for their hospitality towards my daughter Jessica and me. In the middle of my speech, I got down on one knee, took Lisa's hand and asked her to marry me while our families witnessed.

At first she paused and then whispered, "Are you asking me now?" And I said, "Yes, come *on*, will you?" Lisa responded with a big "Yes!" We were married nine months later on April 7, 2002. The ceremony took place in our yard overlooking the lake and our children, Steven and Jessica, were in our wedding, which meant the world to both of us. It was one of the happiest times of my life. Finally, I had the peace of mind I had been searching for all my life and I knew in my heart that Lisa and I would grow old together. Now the time had come for the third stage in my life that Marilyn's guide predicted for me.

The third stage is when you will be on a spiritual path
This is when you are a promoter of God.

Contacting the Departed

Chapter Thirteen

God granted me this gift to communicate with loved ones who have crossed over and it has given me great pleasure to help in the healing process for those who have lost someone. After the loss of a dear friend or loved one, we sometimes wish we could speak with them. While on the earth plane, we sense that the spiritual realm, heaven, is a beautiful and wonderful place. People with near death experiences usually want to stay. But we want to be reassured that our loved ones are okay.

Oftentimes, our loved ones will send us a sign to comfort us shortly after they depart, such as a scent of flowers, tobacco, or perfume, or they will create the sensation of a soft touch on the arm or shoulder. Sometimes we may just sense their presence or we may dream and have visions of our loved ones. They don't want to scare us; they just want us to know that they are fine and still connected to us.

People often ask me how I make contact with spirits. They want to know if the spirit shows its presence to me like the television show, *Ghost Whisperer* or in the movie *Sixth Sense*. I tell them that I am able to bridge the gap between the two planes of existence; that of the living and that of the spirit world. I am *clairsentient*, which simply means clear feeling or the ability to feel the emotions and personalities of the deceased. The deceased will plant a thought, an image, or name into my mind and I will acquire the message from there. After I receive validation that I'm connecting with the deceased person, the information will come through in a straightforward manner. If I contact the departed in a channel state, I will sometimes take on the personality and characteristics of the deceased person.

I prefer to have a small group of people when doing spiritual readings instead of one person, but don't take me wrong; I do personal readings all the time. I just love the energy in the room when it's filled with people. Feeling the love and support of everyone in the room, along with sensing their loved ones comforting them, is a wonderful feeling. When I see mediums on television that fill an auditorium with hundreds and sometime thousands of people wanting to get a reading, I wonder how they do it. I know it takes a tremendous amount of energy to communicate with the other side. When the spirits come through, they want to be heard and recognized. They want to embrace their loved ones and comfort them. There is danger of losing the feeling of love and comfort in a commercialized atmosphere.

People often ask when is the best time to try to connect with our loved ones. Upon losing a loved one, the first thing some grieving people want to do is find a medium so they can contact the deceased. I suggest that you don't do that. As a medium, my best advice is that when a person dies, give them some time before trying to contact them. They, too, are grieving and their spirit needs time to do that and also, to make sure you are okay. An angel, spirit guide or family member will be with them to help them with their grieving and their transition into heaven when it is time for them to move on.

The spirit will attend their own funeral and check on their loved ones day and night. After a few months, the energy of the spirit becomes weak and the memory of the spirit's life on earth begins to fade. They will have a strong desire to go into the light and their angel or guide will direct them through the light and into the astral realm. When passing through the veil, the spirit is rejuvenated with God's energy, making it free and truly bringing it home again. The spirit merges with its higher self (soul) and it's united with its loved ones who have passed over previously, creating a whole new world for them to explore. It is time for them to begin their life in heaven as spirit. The memory of the spirit is restored and it will remember the life it once had and all of its past lives.

Remember that when it is time for you to cross over, your loved ones will be waiting for you to share their lives with you in heaven. In the spirit world, this happens in minutes but and in our world, it's best to wait six to twelve months before contacting the deceased. When doing spiritual readings, I find that usually one to ten years is the best time for contacting spirit because it gives the spirit enough time to settle in. After ten years, the spirit is off doing its own thing and may not want to be contacted, but then again, I have had contact with those whom have passed in as little as a few days. The fact of the matter is it is really up to the spirit to want to make contact with the medium.

Not all Psychics are Mediums, but all Mediums are Psychics.

Three outside sources in the duration of a few days repeated this message to me. My guides really wanted me to know this information. When looking for someone who specializes in contacting the deceased, remember that not all Psychics are Mediums.

A Psychic is someone with second sight, or ESP (Extra Sensory Perception). Some psychics use tools such as Tarot Cards, Runes, Playing Cards or Palmistry. A psychic may also read a person's aura; the energy field that surrounds living things. They use their psychic gifts together with their interpretation skills and knowledge of divination. This gives insight into the inquirer's past, present and potential future. I refer to all Psychics as fortunetellers.

Mediums are people who have a special gift that allows the spirit to give messages from the afterlife. The objective of a medium's work is to prove survival of the human personality after death and to help the bereaved come to terms with their loss. Sittings with mediums are not for fortune telling but are sessions to provide evidence of life after death. Mediumship uses no aids (such as tarot) or interpretative skills. A Mediumistic Reading is a direct intuitive link with the spirit world, the objective being to give proof that we all survive physical death.

A Psychic Medium is someone who works as both a Psychic and a Medium. All true mediums have psychic abilities, anyway, so the term 'Psychic Medium' is somewhat misleading. All Mediums are Psychic. **A Channel Medium** is someone who has the gift of being able to connect with and channel information from Spirit Guides, Angels, and those of the Spirit World. A Channel Medium will receive and translate the information sent by their guides verbally or in writing. This is what I do. Most of the writings in this book are the channeled thoughts from my spirit guides.

When I channel for a group, I become a **Trance Channel**. My guides will merge with me and their personalities will come through. This is why I sometimes pick up the personality of a deceased person. It's like the movie "*Ghost,*" when Sam's spirit merged with the Medium, Oda Mae, and he danced with Molly.

For those of you who have not had the pleasure of attending a Spiritual Reading, I will give you an idea of what to expect. Groups ranging from ten to well over a hundred will meet with me. We dim the lights to enable the spirit to feel comfortable enough to greet their loved ones. I go into a meditation and reach a semi-channeled state. I have no need for a blindfold because when I do my Psychic Medium readings, I do not channel my guides as a trance channel.

Next, I recite one of the protection prayers that I was given by Deborah's guides, to protect everyone in the room from any negativity. I will ask that only the Christ force carrying God's love may come through. I thank God for my gift and for the Collective helping me to connect with the deceased. When connecting with the deceased, my guides will sense each and every person in the room and my guides will connect with your loved ones. The loved ones will translate their message to my guides and then my guides will deliver it to me.

At first I may get a name or an item that, when stated aloud to the group, will be recognized by someone in the group. If I have a large group, I will ask the name of the person that they want to contact. This saves a tremendous amount of time in the process of connecting with the loved one. When we have validation that our loved one is with us, they will bring others in from the family and also friends, to say "Hello." The departed loved ones are with us in the room at times; often I can sense the loved ones draped over someone, giving them the biggest hug. If the energy is strong in the room, you may smell a fragrance. Sometimes you will feel a touch on your shoulder; even the hair on your arms may tingle.

Now that you have an idea of what to expect in a Spiritual Reading, I would like to describe to you a few readings. One reading took place when we had some of my wife's friends over to our home. Previously they'd had had no idea that I was a Psychic Medium since I had been keeping this secret for a long time. At this time, however, I had become more confident in revealing myself. One of Lisa's friends, Sheana, wanted to contact her father who had passed away a little over a year before. Sheana's stepsister, Kim, and Lisa's friends, Liz and Kathleen, came with her for support.

Kathleen is one of my wife's best friends; however, she was very skeptical to learn about what I do, especially since she thought she really knew me. I was just an ordinary 'Joe' to her (so to speak); I came over to watch football, fished with her husband, and did photography for a living. In fact; I was even her wedding videographer when she married Danny. While on their way over to our home, Sheana mentioned to the other women that if I could tell her the pet name her dad called her, then she would be sure that her dad was there.

Since these were her friends, Lisa added a festive air to the spiritual reading night with a wine & cheese party. The women made themselves comfortable in the living room and I sat in front of them in my easy chair. I went into meditation, did my protection prayers, thanked God and the Collective, and began the readings. I asked Sheana her father's name and she told me his name was Kyle. In my mind, I asked my guides to find Kyle and tell him that his daughter was there to greet him.

The first thing that popped into my mind was a pocketknife. I asked for validation from Sheana and she informed me that he had always carried a pocketknife. The next image I received was of a man wearing blue jean suspenders. When I relayed this information to her, Sheana exclaimed, "Oh my God!"

"One year, he tells me now that he hasn't seen you in one year, what is he referring to?" I asked. After some thought, she remembered it had been one year since she visited his grave, so she began to apologize, because he was buried in another state, and she didn't have the means to see him often.

"He wants you to know that it is okay, he understands, and not to worry, Pumpkin." I said. Sheana broke down crying and said, "My dad always called me Pumpkin, which was the pet name I mentioned to everyone while driving over here. I told them that if you said the word 'Pumpkin', then I would know my dad is really here." There was more information. "Your dad tells me that you were named after his sister, Louise." Sheana exclaimed, "Yes, her name was Sheana Louise!"

Sheana asked if her dad remembered the day he died. Sheana's father, Kyle, communicated to me that it was as if he fell asleep, his lungs just stopped. Sheana validated that her dad had died of lung cancer. When she asked if he is ever with her, she was instructed to remember her father's pocket watch that she inherited. "Your father will always be with you when you look at his watch," I told her. "I also sense him in this room, standing by you right now." Sheana thanked me and gave me the biggest hug; it had just meant so much to her to say 'goodbye' to her dad. Lisa was passing tissues out to everyone.

Then I told Kathleen that someone would like to say hello to her; I asked if she was ready. "This person is showing us the 'Philadelphia Eagles' colors and toasting you with a beer, Kathleen; also she is comparing you to Martha Stewart." Everyone began to laugh and Sheana said, "Kathleen, you *are* Martha Stewart," and Lisa agreed.

"This person is showing me a dairy farm that has a creamery; they are making fresh ice cream." Kathleen responded that when she was a child, her grandmom would to take her to Meadow Brook Dairy Farm to buy ice cream. "Now she is showing me a pickle, does this mean anything?" Kathleen replied that her grandmom had pickled everything; she had been known for her pickled food. "Your grandmom is asking about Dean, do you know who he is?" "She might mean my husband, Danny," said Kathleen, laughing. "She could never remember his name!"

"Your grandmom is referring to him as the good-looking one; she says that he is good to my Sunshine." Kathleen started to cry and said, "She always sang that song to me, *You are my Sunshine!*"

"Well, your grandmom wants you to know that she is fine and loves how Danny treats you," I told her. "She also wants me to tell you that you are the apple of her eye and the pie in the sky and she sends you the fragrance of rosemary. She tells me you recognize this smell and will have a warm feeling when you smell the rosemary."

Tears sprang to Kathleen's eyes at this image. But she had another question; she wanted to ask her grandmom if she was mad at her for not being with her when she died. Being a sensitive, I picked up on her grandmom's feelings and repeated her words to Kathleen. "No, no, darling! I can never be mad at my Sunshine. Don't worry; I will never be mad at you." Afterwards, Kathleen thanked me. She told us that her grandmom had called her 'Sunshine' and had often given her warm rosemary-scented baths as a child.

I do things a little bit differently when I connect with the departed while in a channeled state. I blindfold my eyes and recite the protection prayer to myself before I go into a meditation. While I am in meditation, the Collective will connect with me. I thank them for their help and I thank God for this gift. Then Patrick will come through to greet everyone and raise the vibrations in the room.

He will ask individuals from the group for the names of people they would like to contact. After contact is made, the information will come through the Collective. What I channel are the feelings and personality of the deceased and they usually do come through to say hello.

If the Collective feel that someone is in need of spiritual or holistic healing, Indigo will perform this task for the individual who needs it. If that person has any questions about their own journey in life, the Collective will prophesize their future. Now that I have given you an idea about what to expect from a Channeled Spiritual Reading, I would like to describe to you a few Channeled readings:

Another example was another reading for Kathleen. Kathleen's mother in-law, Loraine, had passed away over twelve years before, and she felt that her mother in-law had been murdered. During a Channeled Spiritual Reading, Kathleen asked the Collective if they would contact her. As the information came through from the Collective, here is what they had to say to Kathleen:

Collective: There is the letter M, which Loraine is showing us.

Kathleen: The M stands for Michael, who was the son of my ex-husband and Loraine.

Collective: Is there a grandson who was in the boy scouts and another that played the guitar?

Kathleen: Yes, my nephew, Jody, was in the Boy Scouts and my son, Mark, played the Guitar.

Collective: Loraine is baking pies, does she like to bake?

Kathleen: She loved to bake pies, apple, cherry, you name it!

Collective: Loraine would like to know how Mikey and Markey are.

Kathleen: They are my sons, Mike and Mark, and she always called them Mikey and Markey. Please tell her that they are fine.

Collective: She would like to say hello to George and Missy.

Kathleen: George is her son and Cindy, who she always called Missy, is her daughter.

Kathleen: (Here Kathleen paused and then continued) I would like to know how she died, was it murder?

Collective: She is showing us slippers and her falling down stairs. She tells us that she slipped on the stairs and bled internally.

Kathleen: They found her in bed the next day with blood draining from her mouth. We weren't sure if she was pushed or had fallen on her own. Thank you clearing things up.

This is from a reading for my teacher Marilyn. She wanted to contact Linda, who had passed away in 1966; Marilyn wanted to know if she had a message from Linda.

Collective: Time will heal all wounds and don't sweat the small stuff. Does this mean anything to you?

Marilyn: I sweat the small stuff everyday of my life. Ask Linda when I think of her, why do I think of Silent Night?

Collective: It is the still of the night, a night of peace, trinity, holiness and being together as one; to be united with the Father.

Marilyn: Is she okay with the thought about how she died?

Collective: We see an amputation, a removal, this is how she died. It was a shock!

Marilyn: She was decapitated.

Collective: Yes, this is what she meant; time did heal all wounds.

Marilyn: She died on Christmas Eve.

Collective: The oneness, to be with the Father and the still of the night.

Marilyn: We always sang Silent Night.

Collective: We bless everyone here tonight and express our love and devotion to each one of you.

As a final note in this chapter, I would like to thank all of the readers for sharing this gift with me. It was foretold to me many years ago that I was to become a Medium to those who have departed, and a Channel of Spirit Guides. I thank God to have this honor and gift bestowed on me. I also would like to thank Liz Sterling, founder & director of *Life Works* of Boca Raton, Florida, and Ronnie Guenther, director of operations, for being the first to give me the opportunity to share my gift by allowing me to have a "Messages from Heaven Gallery" at their healing center.

Mama Always Said I was Psychic

Chapter Fourteen

Ever since I was a child, my mother always insisted that I had a gift. She used to tell me that I always had a knack for knowing things that were about to happen before they happened. As I got older I tended to ignore my gift; it wasn't until I was an adult that it began to surface again. For years my mother was my biggest - and only - fan. She would have me predict things that were going to happen in the world and would ask about her family. Every time something I predicted came true, my mother would be on the phone to me, encouraging me to accept the fact that my gifts were real and that I should use them to help others.

To be honest with you, when I was younger I was the type of guy who would make fun of psychics. I would poke fun along with my dad when my mother would tell us about her Grandmother Francesca and my Uncle Jose, both of whom were renowned as gifted psychics. Still, I played along with my mom, giving her readings because it seemed to give her peace of mind. I'd like to take this opportunity to say, "Mom, I have to admit that I was wrong and I apologize to you and all of the psychics in the world!"

It took me years, but I have accepted my gift and have come to terms with what I do. Even my father, who was the biggest skeptic in the world, has become a fan of my abilities. Lisa and my mother convinced my dad to attend one of my "Messages from Heaven" Gallery and Book Signing events. There was a crowd of over a hundred people who looked eager to get messages from their loved ones, but I could see one face in the crowd that really stood out. It was my dad and, boy, he did not what to be there!

As the event began, I was introduced to the crowd and was welcomed with applause. I launched into my psychic medium thing, similar to a John Edwards "Crossing Over" gallery. As the messages poured in from the loved ones and as I was communicating them to a receptive and grateful crowd, I could see that my dad was actually smiling! He'd finally realized that what I did is not mysterious or weird; I wasn't dressed in robes and there was no crystal ball. To my dad, I was an entertainer. The messages that came through brought in tears and laughter from the audience; there were a lot of heartfelt and loving messages that came through that evening. Afterwards, as I was signing books for the audience members, my dad came up to me and admitted that for years he had the wrong impression about what I did. He wanted me to know that he now supported me in my accomplishments and endeavors.

My guides had always urged me to have patience; to know that this book would be published and well-loved. Well, as usual, The Collective was right. I have received great feedback on how much readers have enjoyed the book and it has opened many new doors for me. My galleries and book signings have been a great success. I'm doing readings all over the world and made the Top Psychic Medium list by Mediumchannel.com. I've also experienced several radio appearances. It gives me great satisfaction that I can make an impact on people's lives and that I am able to help people cope with the death of their loved ones or with their direction in life.

When I receive messages from the other side from our loved ones, I find that I also get messages from the spirit guides or angels of the person whom I'm reading. For years I just refused to do psychic readings. I felt that everyone has free will and that if I predicted something, a person could always change the outcome. Well, this all can be true, but on the other hand, I might have been wrong about not passing on the psychic messages. I began to take note of the positive feedback I received when my predictions came true. I realized that I must also provide this service to others based on all of the people who thanked me for helping them find clarity and direction in their lives and I finally decided to embrace my gift instead of denying it.

What really set my mind to this was an experience that I had with a psychic, Linda Ireland, who works at a New Age bookstore called *Spiritual Awakenings* in Lantana Florida. Linda came to me for a reading to connect with her departed loved ones, but for some reason I had a hard time connecting. Instead I was getting other information pertaining to her. I asked her who Allen was and she'd replied that he was her brother, but he was still alive.

I passed the next impression I got on to her: "I'm getting something about running out of time, does this makes sense?" She shook her head no. I asked her if the song, "*Wakeup Little Suzy*" meant anything. Linda told me that she had no idea what I was talking about. At this point I wanted to give up, thinking that I was making a fool of myself, but I kept on telling her what I was seeing. "I now see you in a Trans Am on the highway, just like the movie *Smokey and the Bandit.*" Again she said "Nope! I don't own a Trans Am and never had one in my life!"

She looked frustrated. After that response, I had to stop and apologize to her, but I thanked her for having faith in me. For some reason I'd had a hard time reaching her loved ones and nothing I said to her made sense. I even called her the next day asking her if maybe I could give her another reading some other time; that I just might have had an off day. Linda told me not to worry, that maybe her loved ones weren't ready to come through.

Well, a couple of days later Linda called and said "Joe, you mentioned my brother Allen and running out of time. Well, my brother Allen passed away this morning. I began to think back when we were kids and we used to tear up the dance floor together and one of our favorite songs was *Wakeup Little Suzy.*" As I expressed sympathy at the death of her brother, Linda praised me on my gift. Neither of us realized at the time that more information from the reading was going to come true.

Linda's children didn't want her driving her old pick up truck up north to her brother's funeral and asked their father, Linda's ex-husband, to loan her his car. When Linda arrived at his house to pick up the car, there in the driveway sat a Pontiac Firebird that looked like a Trans Am. The only thing missing from the car was the Trans Am stickers!

Later, as she was driving north on I- 95 Linda was thinking about calling me about the car and wasn't paying attention to how fast she was driving. A semi-truck in front of her started to slow down and she had to slow down as well. As she decided to go around the truck that was in front of her, another semi pulled up next her and prevented her from passing. As she looked through her review mirror, another truck pulled up behind her, effectively boxing her in. She began to feel nervous, thinking that theses truckers were playing games. As soon as she had an opening she hit the gas to escape the trucks and they all laid down on their horns. This is when Linda noticed a line of state troopers pulling speeders over. Finally, she realized that the truckers were only slowing her down for her own benefit, just like in the movie *Smokey and the Bandit*. After hearing the events that unfolded with Linda, I decided to accept my psychic abilities.

Incidentally, Linda has been very helpful in teaching me the finer techniques of presenting psychic readings to the public. Instead of just using telepathy with my guides, she advised me that the public is accustomed to the tools typically used by psychics such as tarot cards, the use of a crystal ball, or a pendulum for 'yes' and 'no' answers. Through use of these tools of the trade when doing a reading, the client is focused on the tools and not on me. I'd still be receiving the information from my guides but using the tools puts on a good show for the client.

I bought a deck of tarot cards and wasted a night memorizing the definition of each card and how to lay them out. Then Linda had me return the deck for one that was more artistic with colorful drawings. She instructed me to look at the pictures on the cards and let them tell me a story. Eventually I found that after staring at the pictures for awhile, they came to life and the told me a story about the person's life. In this manner, it really works. Linda has been a great help and I thank her for putting me on the right path in learning the techniques of doing a psychic reading.

The Collective Way of Thinking

Although I tried using the tarot cards in readings, I found myself thinking too much instead of letting the information come to me like when I do my spirit readings. Indigo made me realize that I had not trusted my ability; I was using the cards as a crutch. So I came to terms with myself on how to do my readings and what works for me. As a psychic, I do not use any tools such as tarot cards, astrology or photos.

I receive information by telepathy directly from my guides. During the course of the reading, I'm able to see opportunities and obstacles in your path whether they are in your past, present or future. When a client asks me a question, the Collective will take me back to the point in their past where the root of the problem had begun. During a reading I will notice disturbances in the person's energy throughout their life and will ask what has happened in this year or that year. Please realize that absolutely **no** psychic can see your future as one hundred percent set in stone; if they say that they can they are not telling you the truth.

When doing a reading, I provide insight on paths you may take and the opportunities and obstacles that may be presented to you. Remember that God gave us free will and the choice is always yours to make. So if you decide that path "B" would be better then path "A", then the Law of Attraction will become activated and you will attract the future from the chosen path. We are on a journey in life and thought is reality, so your thoughts create your own future. Your life is the result of a series of choices presented to you, and the decisions that you make based on those choices.

Psychic Development

Lisa had been working on her own psychic abilities and had gotten pretty good. (Maybe it's because she has a great teacher)! I had reconnected with my mentor, Marilyn, and she has helped both of us tremendously. Marilyn watched me grow through the years and is very proud of my accomplishments.

The classes that I had taken from Marilyn inspired me to teach an Intuitive Development class of my own. Lori and Roger, the owners of a New Age store in Royal Palm Beach, Florida, called *The Witch's Hat*, gave me the opportunity to teach such a class. Mary, one of the psychics at *The Witch's Hat*, helped me with direction on how to teach the class. The students were very eager to learn. Through teaching the class I have found that all of them had psychic abilities; it just took learning how to open their sixth sense. (It helps when you have a class full of wonderful students, too)!

I start out the class with an exercise called "Mind Send". I have a person stand in front of the group holding flashcards with various shapes and have them focus mentally to project the shape on the card to each person in the class with their mind. The lesson in this exercise is to learn how to project your thoughts to others; it's a form of telepathy or Extrasensory Perception (ESP). Next, I pair up the group and have them face one another with hands held, left palm up and right palm down. Having their hands positioned in this way keeps the flow of energy circling between them. This exercise is called "Hands-on Psychometry" and the lesson is how to access a form of telepathy by vibration. While holding hands, partner number one will send a specific message, such as a number, by telepathy to partner number two. You would be surprised at how many people get the right answers once they're opened up to it.

The most popular exercise we do is "Psychometry by Touch". I have everyone place an object that they have in their possession into a basket. The objects are re-distributed so that no one knows who owns the object they each randomly select to read. By holding the object they drew, the person will begin to receive impressions about the person who owns the object, like how their day went or what they have eaten that day.

A great tool that we use in the reading is a Numerology Chart; it can be used as a sort of cheat sheet. The chart lists attributes that are associated with these numbers, such as Leadership for the number one or Spirituality for the number seven. The chart serves as a sort of 'psychic short-hand' so that the person performing the reading needs only to concentrate on opening up to receive the number. The reader can then refer to the chart for the meaning. (I have mine memorized to help me when I do psychic readings for a person). I have my students hold the object in their hand and I ask them to "see" a number in their mind that is on the numerology chart. The number they see in their mind represents traits and characteristics of the person for whom they are reading.

To give you an example, let's say we hold the object and we "see" the number four in our mind. The number four on the numerology chart stands for Routine and represents a hard worker, discipline and creating a foundation. On a challenging note it can mean lazy, stubborn and set in their ways; also, grouchy and having a fixed opinion. So this is how I would do a reading for that person. "I feel that you are a very routine person that needs things to be in order. You work hard to get where you are in life at and are very disciplined. However, you can be very stubborn and set in your ways." You will be surprised at how accurately you can give a reading by using this numerology chart. I included a chart for you to use on the next page. Give it a try and impress your friends with your psychic abilities!

Numerology Chart

#1 Leadership- a new beginning, pioneer, showing leadership, forceful, being original, cheerful & hopeful.
Challenge- Overly independent, selfish, aggressive know it all.

#2 Patience- Idealistic collector, consideration, cooperation, sensitive.
Challenge- Inferiority. Lack self-confidence shy, easy to walk over.

#3 Creativity - communication, beauty, romantic, loving, self-expression.
Challenge- Jealousy, gossip, talk too much.

#4 Routine - hard worker, routine, discipline creating a foundation
Challenge- Lazy, stubborn, grouchy, fixed opinion.

#5 Change- transition, freedom, optimistic, surprises.
Challenge- Restless, overindulgent, accident-prone.

#6 Giving- Family oriented, home, domestic, responsible Love of beauty & harmony
Challenge -Selfishness in home & relationship sympathetic to take on troubles.

#7 Spiritual- learning, understanding, self-analysis, clever, love of nature, science minded natural healers.
Challenge- Very aloof, shy, sarcastic, many challenges, false pride.

#8 Power- Successful, business oriented, total control, world in your hands.
Challenge- Materialistic, love of power ruthless in power, money important.

#9 Separation- get rid of things, out with the old in with the new, compassionate, humanitarian, giving.
Challenge- Emotional, bad temper, vulgar, never take responsibilities for actions,

#11 Intuitive- Open to the universe, Fame, good intuition, divine.
Challenge- Dishonest, self-center, thief, lack understanding.

#22 Universal- Director of World affairs, efficiency expert, manifestation, uplifting
*Challenge- **(same as eleven)** Dishonest, self-center, thief, lack understanding.*

There are many techniques in psychic development, but to be good at it you must practice. It's like learning a musical instrument for the first time; you must ***practice, practice, and practice***! This is how I teach my workshops. The more we study the fundamentals of psychic development, the more open we become.

Mediumship Cafe

I was asked to be a guest speaker for a group called *Mediumship Cafe* that met at the "Inner Wisdom," a bookstore in Deerfield Beach. The group organizer, Laura Mendelsohn, is also a psychic medium. She invited me to talk about my channeling and to demonstrate my mediumship abilities to the class. I would have fifteen minutes to talk about myself and my book and to answer questions. When I asked Laura for permission to sell my books, she referred me to the storeowner, Dottie. As I was speaking with Dottie, I also asked her to give me an idea of how many might attend and to see how many books to bring.

Since the mediumship class was new, she thought that there might only be a few people and that ten books would be enough. Ha! Normally I would take more time to prepare before doing a gallery or speaking at any function, but I was thinking that there would only be a small group, so it would be no big deal. I even dressed down for the occasion in my shorts and flip-flops, but luckily, as I was on my way out the door, Lisa stopped me and made me dress as if I were going to do a regular gallery. Usually Lisa will attend a gallery with me to give me support but I told her to stay home this time - this would be a small group and I'd be back home shortly.

As I walked into the store I thought, 'Wow, this is a happening place!' The store was filled with people looking at books and gifts. I found Laura in the back room surrounded by many empty chairs. She said that the session would begin in about fifteen minutes and told me to make myself comfortable. She told me that she was going to play a video on mediumship first before she introduced me to the room. I made my way to the back row of chairs to take a seat. Quickly the room filled up with people as one after another came in to find a seat. Soon all of the chairs were taken and people lined up against the wall; I wondered were all of these people had come from!

I felt as though I were in disguise because no one knew who I was, nor did I recognize anyone from the group. I just sat with the crowd and listened to Laura's presentation.

After she finished, Laura pointed me out and told the group that I would be demonstrating my mediumship abilities to them. As all eyes turned to me, I had that "deer caught in headlights" feeling. This was not my regular crowd, nor were they the average person who wanted to hear from a loved one. They were all practicing psychic mediums, so this was essentially a group of my peers. As we watched the short movie on mediumship, I began to worry and to think, "Who am I to be here demonstrating *my* abilities to all of these psychic mediums?"

I should always have faith in my guides. After the movie Laura introduced me to the crowd and I began my gallery. The first to come in was a man who said he had played ball; not major league baseball but in the minors. At first, no one claimed him; the room was a study in silence. It was so quiet that I could hear the breathing of every person in the room. So I continued to pass on more information that the spirit was telling me. He had only passed away a short time ago; it may have been only a few weeks. He had lived in the Northeast and the team he had played for was the Dodgers – but not the Los Angeles Dodgers; he had played for them when they were still in New York and they were called the Brooklyn Dodgers.

Now I got someone attention! A voice from the back of the room said, "You must have connected with my grandfather!" Her name is Deirdre Abrami; a psychic medium and intuitive who, it turns out, hosts a weekly local radio show called *"The Angel Hour"*. Deirdre identified the spirit as her grandfather who just passed away only two weeks prior. As I blew her a kiss from grandpa just the way he used to kiss her goodbye, it made a strong validation for her that it was him. That opened the door for many more loved ones to come in for the group; many others received messages. I was told afterwards that I had made a great impression on everyone. I was further honored that Deirdre invited me to be a guest on her radio show the following month.

Mediumship 101

That night I learned a different approach to mediumship as taught to Deirdre. This technique had to do with working with the aura around a person's body. I took a course with Deirdre a few months later to learn of this technique to become certified myself. During class we learned of the "**Four -Clair's**":

Clairaudient: the psychic ability to hear beyond the range of the normal human hearing.

Clairsentient: clear feeling – the ability to psychically feel the emotions and personalities of the deceased.

Clairvoyance: the psychic ability to see things beyond the range of normal human vision.

Claircognizance: translates to "clear knowingness"; this is an ability to just know things without conventional sensory input; no one tells you, you just *know* it.

In Deirdre's mediumship course we also learned that you must complete three steps in order to have validation that you are connected to a loved one.

1. **Identify**
2. **One Fact**
3. **Message of Love**

The best way to describe how this works is to tell you about how my reading went. My partner Janet approached me and used her hands to sense the energy around my body. Her hands hovered above my head and began to favor more of the left side (facing her). She asked if I had a father in spirit and I told her that my father in-law had recently passed away, so that was the first step to identify the loved one. Next, she told me that she saw him as being always on his knees did this make sense?

It certainly did. Lisa's father, Douglas Murray, had passed away in December 2007. He had lived with us so that Lisa and I could take care of him. Doug had Parkinson's, which is why he had lost his ability to walk on his own and he would always fall to the ground "on his knees" when he tried.

The final step is a loving message. Janet told me, "Doug wants you to know that it's everything that you said. The door opened and my family was there to greet me. Thank you, Joe and Lisa, for everything you have done for me!" I was in tears, I was so happy to receive this message. Since he had died, I had tried to channel Doug for Lisa, but it's hard to channel family members for yourself. The message that Janet passed to me meant so very much. It also made me realize how my work as a medium must effect others in the same way.

So that's how it works. First, you place your hands around the upper half of the body of the person you are reading and try to sense an intense feeling of heat or a tingle. Once you can sense this and you have established where the energy is, there is a basic pattern of who that entity is in relation to the person. For example, a father energy will come in above and to the left of them. (*I have included a chart below so you too can learn this mediumship technique and have a better understanding of how to do a mediumistic reading*).

Next, listen for or feel what the spirit is saying and come up with a fact to validate that you are connecting. And finally, listen for a loving message from the loved one and pass it on. This is a great technique for those who want to learn the basics of mediumistic readings. Practice with your friends and see how it all works!

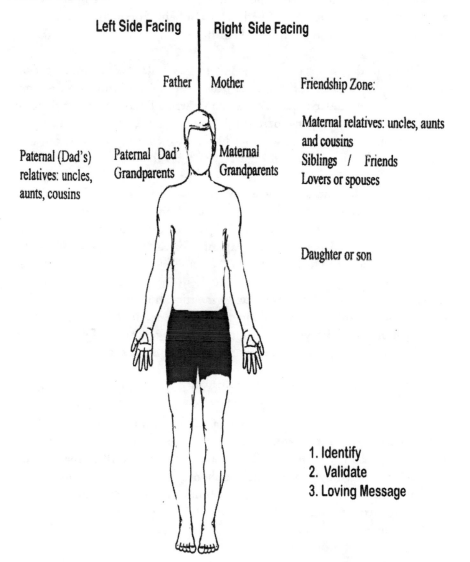

Left Side Facing | **Right Side Facing**

Father | Mother

Friendship Zone:

Maternal relatives: uncles, aunts and cousins
Siblings / Friends
Lovers or spouses

Paternal (Dad's) relatives: uncles, aunts, cousins

Paternal Dad' Grandparents

Maternal Grandparents

Daughter or son

1. Identify
2. Validate
3. Loving Message

On the Radio

The next challenge in my career was doing psychic readings on the radio. Deirdre Abrami, host of *"The Angel Hour"*, whom I had met in the mediumship class, gave me the first opportunity for a radio appearance.

It was Halloween night and for some reason; I thought it would be a slow night since people would be busy with the trick or treaters who would be out in full force. It wasn't; in fact, the phone lines lit up like a Christmas tree and, wow, was I ever nervous! I had visions of being tongue-tied and having nothing to say, but with the help of Deirdre and my wife, I pulled it off.

Giving readings over the radio is not an easy task. During an in-person reading or phone reading, if I need to pause to receive information from my guides, the client understands. But if I pause while I'm on the radio, I create dead air space and boring radio, so this is something I resolved to work on for future media appearances. It was nice having my wife cheering me on; Lisa helped me to keep my cool and I did very well for the first time on the air.

The first caller was a man who had never spoken to a psychic medium. He asked if there were any loved ones around him. I got the letter "R" and asked him what it stood for; it could be a place or title. For awhile that made no sense; however, I got something about a pastor and asked, "Who's the pastor?" and then it all made sense. The "R" stood for "Reverend" - his father had indeed been a great pastor and the founder of over one hundred churches throughout South Florida. I went on to mention how many years his father had been gone and how many siblings he had. Since it was radio, our time was cut short, but I knew I had so much more to tell him - if we had more time! Afterwards, he thanked me for the authenticity of my work.

When I connected with the last caller of the evening, I felt a feeling of sorrow and remorse. I knew that she had lost a child. The impression that came to my mind was that it had been a young man and that he had been at the wrong place at the wrong time. Two people were involved; I got the sense that he had been murdered by gunshot. The caller verified that her son had been murdered by gunshot and the shooter had then turned the gun on himself, making it a murder-suicide. I told the caller how much her son loved her and missed her and that he was truly sorry for all of the pain she was going through.

Time sure flies when on you're the radio, but what a great experience. The lines fill up with callers and it seems that we always run out of time before we can talk to everyone. Since my first appearance, Deirdre has had me on several more times as a regular. I like it so much that I now host my own radio show *Journey Of Life Radio*.

Angels and Spirit Guides

Chapter Fifteen

Hello again, this is Genevieve. I would like to talk about Angels. The purpose of Angels in life is to serve the one and only God. We have our jobs to do, just like every one of you do. My purpose is to bring forth the wisdom of God through messengers like Joseph. Many scribes that wrote the bible channeled the wisdom of God from the Angels and Spirit Guides; they were known as the messengers of God.

Just as you have a governmental political system to enforce the laws; we, too, have a hierarchy of Angels that oversee everything; they are known as the Archangels. God appointed these Angels to keep balance in the universe. The Archangels have specific areas of responsibilities where they oversee all of God's creations.

God appointed **Archangel Michael** as the Warrior Angel of Light who would lead the celestial army of angels to protect the light from darkness. Archangel Michael is the right hand of God, always on guard, always protecting the Souls from negativity. Archangel Michael governs a legion of angels to protect the light from darkness.

God appointed **Archangel Raphael** as the Healing Angel. The healing vibration is directed through Archangel Raphael whenever the soul or the spirit body is in need of healing. Archangel Raphael governs a legion of angels to assist with the healers of your world.

God appointed **Archangel Uriel** as the Angel of the Light. Archangel Uriel is the bringer of the light to all souls. God's wisdom and inspiration are delivered through the Archangel Uriel. Archangel Uriel governs a legion of angels to assist with distributing the light of God throughout the universe. I, Genevieve, report to The Archangel Uriel. The wisdom and inspiration of God is given to me through the Archangel Uriel. I relay messages to the Channel Mediums who are like Joseph.

God appointed **Archangel Gabriel** as the Messenger Angel. Known as the voice of God, the Angel Gabriel appeared to Mary, the Blessed Mother, and Joseph. The voice from the heavens that announced to the people, "Christ has risen," was the voice of Gabriel. Archangel Gabriel governs the legion of angels whose messages are expressed through the seers and prophets of your world.

Have you ever given thought to the Fallen Angels of God? Was there a rebellion in heaven that made God cast out some of his angels? **The Fallen Angel, Lucifer,** was once the closest Archangel to God. The name Lucifer means "the bringer of the light." Lucifer had a great desire to experience life, much like humans do. He wanted free will and choice and to be a co-creator of life. Lucifer wanted to experience the emotions of pleasure and pain. He looked to the earth with envy and this was appealing to Lucifer.

God understood what Lucifer wanted. Out of God's love, He granted Lucifer permission to experience life. God warned Lucifer that when he left heaven he would forget the privileges and the knowledge of heaven, and he would be alone. Lucifer did not want to be alone so he banded together with his legion of angels and persuaded them to go with him. He also convinced some of the angels that were in allegiance with the other Archangels to join him. This caused a division in heaven and the Archangel Michael battled with Lucifer, to keep him from recruiting more angels. God at first refrained, but out of love for Lucifer and his angels, God decided to let Lucifer take his legions of angels into the lower realms.

God warned Lucifer and the angels again, "When you leave this place and pass through the veil, you cannot return, and as the time passes on, you will lose all memory of heaven." But the angels were determined, and they left heaven. The angels fell through the veil into the lower realms, losing most memory of who they were and of God. When they arrived in the earthly realm, the angels became disenchanted with the earth. They wanted to return to the grandeur of God and his infinite source of love and light, but they had lost their way home. The fallen angels became part of the earth and created the duality of good and evil. Lucifer and his legion of fallen angels surrendered to the illusion of the physical world along with having materialistic goals.

The more successful Lucifer and the fallen angels were at persuading the "Spirit of Light" to turn from God and become dark, the more powerful Lucifer and the fallen angels felt. The last battle will be when the New Age is upon you; this will be the battle between good and evil. The Archangel Michael and Lucifer will battle once more, and at the end of this battle, the good will prevail and the fallen angels will return home to God to take their rightful place. God will be merciful to Lucifer and welcome His defiant son.

God appointed **Guardian Angels** to overlook people from the day they are born until their death. These angels help us and protect us throughout our lives. I, Genevieve, am a Guardian Angel to Joseph, and have stepped in many times to keep him from harm's way. I was with him when he rolled his van many years ago.

Joseph was driving south-bound on the Florida Turnpike on a stormy, rainy day, returning from a trip in Indiana. The driver of a northbound vehicle lost control of his car, slid across the grass median, and smashed into Joseph's van. The van started to roll and Joseph's seatbelt became unfastened, but I, along with other angels, held him suspended in the air while his vehicle rolled around him a few times. The van stopped rolling and was lying on the driver's side. Joseph climbed out of the passenger window and walked away with only a cracked watch crystal!

People that are killed from accidents die because of events that are related to their karma; it was planned before the birth of the individual. If the accidents are not karma-related, or planned, the Guardian Angel will be there to rescue them. Have you have ever changed your mind all of the sudden, without reason, because you had a feeling? Your Guardian Angel properly advised you to change your mind. By using your intuition, you connected with your Guardian Angel.

When you think of **Angels,** you envision glowing halos and giant wings, but in reality, you will never know who or where they are. It might be someone on the street or a person you meet briefly. We will show ourselves as humans only to blend in. We are here to help and bring God's love, so the next time you meet a loving stranger, give some thought that you might have met an angel. Thank you for your divine attention, and remember that the angels are watching over all of you.

Until we meet again - **Genevieve**

Spirit Guides

Greetings; it is I, Indigo! Now it is time to inform you about the purpose of having Spirit Guides. When Joseph channels, he is not channeling the spirits of the loved ones who have departed, he is connecting to his Spirit Guides. Spirit Guides are entities, or beings, that are currently in the spirit realm or dimensions. These are individuals, or groups of individuals, who have agreed with a person on the earth plane to act as their guide or guardian. Usually we enter into this agreement with at least one "primary guide", called the control, prior to being born into a physical body.

It is not uncommon to have two or more guides assisting us at a given moment. Many of the guides with whom we work are beings that have lived on this earth plane at one time or another (or many lifetimes) but there are guides who are from other worlds as well. Also, many of the "special guides" that come to help us with special needs or learning experiences are usually more evolved beings, or 'old souls' who willingly share their expertise and expanded knowledge with those of us still working on our path to enlightenment.

Spirit Guides really love the laughter of people. They like to come close and enjoy the physical sensation of laughter, like Patrick, who is known for his laughter. These Guides are known as the **Joy Guides;** they will bring harmony and the laughter. There are also guides that are very **Old and Wise;** these Master Guides have been around the earth a long time. These Guides are the ones to teach of the early biblical times. The Ancient One is to bring information to Joseph of biblical times.

There are **Guides to the children.** These guides love the children; they are the invisible playmates that children insist they can see or hear. Genevieve came through to talk with Joseph's daughter, Jessica, when she was a child. The American Indians were people who worshiped the earth; the **Indian Guides** taught the knowledge of their oneness with all life, to be one with Mother Earth. Sparrow Hawk is the guide bringing information of the earth to Joseph.

Healing Guides are the ones to bring in the healing energy of God. I, Indigo, am the one who brings in the healing through Joseph. It is impossible to categorize all of the guides; the Collective are a group of infinite number of guides that Joseph will channel in his journeys.

From Joseph: The Spirit Guides have helped me to have direction in my life. The wisdom and teachings of the Collective has brought me closer to God and understanding my own journey in life. They have made it possible for me to channel the wisdom and love from the Master himself Jesus. It gives me great pleasure to be the channel for Jesus' wisdom in the next chapter.

The Promise

Chapter Sixteen

Greetings, everyone, from Patrick on behalf of the Collective. We would like to inform you, dear readers, of the Christ Consciousness. (For some, this will be a reminder).

God created the world with the light of Christ. The Christ energy is one of the highest vibrations known. To be a part of the Christ Consciousness is the highest award the Creator can give to a being. Honors are bestowed to Abraham, Moses, Joshua and Jesus, to name a few. This energy was a part of the Master called Jesus. This is why he was known as The Christ. The Christ Consciousness will return once again to earth in the New Age. We will explain later on about the New Age, but for now we would like to take you back two thousand years to the birth of Jesus.

Who was this man called The Christ?

His name in Aramaic is Yeshua; he was known as Jesus of Nazareth, the man from Galilee, who eventually became known as "Jesus the Christ".

What does *The Christ* mean? The word Christ itself is from the Greek word Kristos and means "the anointed" (the same definition of the Hebrew word "Messiah"). Every anointed person is Christed. The Collective is part of the Christ Consciousness, for we are Christed; we are anointed with the Christ Force. The Christ is the only Son by the Almighty God. Without the Christ, there would be no light. Through Him all things were made; and so through Him things were done. This man called Jesus Christ was the very eternal God, clothed in the flesh of man so that men would witness his glory.

"I am here for my Father to open your eyes. About our Father-Mother God: There are no other Gods; only our Creator is God; remember, I am not God, I am the Son of God. The Creator has sent me to cleanse the earth of all its sins. I am to return your memory of who is and what is God, for He is Love and Hope for mankind. Follow me to His Kingdom, and He will grant you everlasting life. Follow my footsteps into the light of pure love. Open your hearts to Him, the Lord, our God. Feel the goodness inside when the energy of God is around you. I am Jesus, the channel to the Creator of pure love. I am the channel of this love energy. I am the channel to all of our Father's Creations. First, you must believe and have faith in our Father God. Then you will receive the blessing and the love of that there is."

("What's the matter, Joseph? Why did you stop writing?" asked Patrick. "Did you channel that message to me?" I asked him. "No, Joseph. Haven't we, the Collective, informed you that you will be a reporter to the Christ? Remember that you are a part of the Christ Consciousness. You are now a part of the Collective. You knew Jesus when he was a being on earth and He remembers the kindness and support you gave to Him. So do not be surprised if He channels messages through you; it will not be the last time. We are only at the beginning of your journey, now may we begin with his amazing story)?"

The Metaphysical Story of Jesus Christ

In the hills of Judea lived a priest by the name of Zachariah, along with his wife, Elizabeth. One day when Zachariah entered the sanctuary to pray, the angel Gabriel appeared to him and said, *"Oh man of God, fear not; I bring to you and all of the world a message of good will. Your wife, Elizabeth, will bear you a son, of whom the prophets wrote. Behold, I send unto you Elijah again, before the coming of our Lord. He will pave the way for the Prince of Peace, the King you seek; from his birth he will be filled with the Holy Spirit, and will be known as John."*

Time passed. Now the angel Gabriel visited Mary, who was engaged to Joseph, son of Jacob, a carpenter by trade, in Galilee. *"Greetings, favored one!"* proclaimed the angel. *"Do not be afraid. You are blessed in the name of God; blessed in the name of the Holy Spirit; and blessed in the name of Christ, for you are worthy, and will bear a son whom you shall call 'Yeshua', to be known to all as 'Jesus'. He will save the people from their sins."*

As it was foretold, Mary was great with child. Mary and Joseph traveled to the hills of Judea to pay a visit to Elizabeth and Zachariah. As they were on their way, they came to Bethlehem and needed to stop for the night to rest. Bethlehem was crowded with multitudes of people going into Jerusalem; the inns were filled with guests and Joseph and Mary could not find an inn. They found a place to rest in a cave, where the beasts of burden were kept.

At midnight, there came a voice from the heavens above. An angel appeared above the cave and said, *"A child is born in yonder cave where the animals are kept, he sleeps in a manger where the beasts of burden are fed."* Three wise men, following the brightly lit star, came across the cave in Bethlehem. They stood before the child and said, *"All strength, wisdom and love are yours, Emmanuel, you in whom God is with us."* As the shepherds, too, came close to the shimmering light, an angel appeared and announced to them, *"Fear not! Behold, I bring you joyful news. At midnight in this cave was born a prophet and a king that you have long waited for. All glory to God on high; peace on earth; good will to men!"*

Joseph sent word to Zachariah and Elizabeth that their child had been born in Bethlehem. Zachariah and his wife took their son, John, and went to Bethlehem. After eight days passed, Jesus was to be consecrated. According to the laws of Moses, when the time came for purification, they brought Jesus to Jerusalem to present him to the Lord. A man by the name of Simeon was at the temple and asked to see the child. He had prayed to God that he would see the Messiah in the flesh. And so it was; he took the child in his arms and said, *"Behold, this child Yeshua will bring a sword upon my people of Israel, and the world; but he will break the sword and then the nation will learn war no more. Behold, our King!"*

A ruler of Judea by the name of King Herod was told of the child ordained to become King. He called into council his Jewish masters of law and asked, "What have the prophets said of the one called Emmanuel?" He was told that the prophets of long ago foretold of the One who would come and rule all of Israel; that this Messiah would be born in Bethlehem in the land of Judea. King Herod thought to himself, "Such a prophecy shall not happen, no one will have claimant upon my throne!" King Herod was also told of another child in Bethlehem; one who had been born to go before the Messiah and prepare the people to receive the King. This enraged King Herod even more. He called in his guards. "Go into Bethlehem and slay the infant John as well as the one called Jesus, who was born King," he commanded them. "And make no mistake; slay all male children in the town that are not two years of age!" Word came to Joseph and Mary of the infant slayings, so they collected their things, took the infant Jesus, and fled to Egypt. The guards went forth and did as King Herod commanded them to do. Elizabeth also knew of King Herod's intention to slay her son John, so she took him into the hills of Judea to hide in the caves. They hid until the cruel task of the guards was done. When the guards returned to King Herod, they informed him of the slaying of all the infants who were under two years of age. A council was called of the wisest men in King Herod's court. He asked them about the infant claimant to his throne. The council informed King Herod that the infants John and Jesus were both dead, so King Herod was satisfied.

Joseph and Mary remained for awhile in Egypt with their son Jesus, where they resided with a man who was a master of God's teachings. Word came to Joseph that King Herod had put his friend Zachariah to death for not revealing the whereabouts of his son John. Elizabeth was still in the hills of Judea in hiding with the infant John. Joseph hastily sent messages until Elizabeth and John were found and brought to Egypt. Elizabeth and John were reunited with Joseph's family. Mary and Elizabeth asked the master with whom they had sought refuge what was to become of their children, Jesus and John.

The master laid his hand on the shoulders of both women and said to them, "It is not strange that you are both here in this sacred place at this time. From olden times it was ordained that you should be with us, it is prophecy. You are both blessed, for you are both chosen mothers of long promised sons. They will lay a foundation that will support the perfect man and here shall rest a temple that will never be destroyed. No man lives unto himself, for every living thing is connected to every other living thing. Bless the one who is pure in heart, for he will love unconditionally. They will do unto other men what is done to them.

"Man was created in two selves, the higher and the lower. The Lower Self, the carnal self, is full of desire and untruths. It breeds hatred, wars and mistrust. It is only flesh and bone that will decay; it is an illusion and will soon pass away. The Higher Self is God in man and will not pass away. It is truth, justice, and love. The Higher Self is of spirit that is of soul, made in the form of God.

"As we measure time in cycles, a new age is upon us. As an age passes, the gates open for a new age to begin. This new age is the preparation of the soul, the kingdom of Emmanuel, of God within us. Your sons will be the first to welcome this age, to tell the news and teach of God, peace on earth, goodwill to men. A mighty work is set forth for them to be the deliverers of the Light. Men on earth live in the dark and do not know the meaning of one who is of Light. Your sons are here to bring the Light unto all of mankind. First, they must have the Light before they can reveal it. You must teach your sons and make them aware of their missions to the son of men.

"Teach them that God and man are one; but through carnal thoughts, man tore himself away from God. Teach that the Spirit of Christ will make them whole again by restoring harmony and peace. God so loved the world that he clothed his only Son in flesh, so that man will understand that the Savior of the world is Love. Jesus comes to man to teach of love. And Elizabeth, you are blessed with a son of purity, made of flesh. He shall pave the way for love. This age will be an age that will comprehend the works of purity and love. A mighty work is given unto you. You shall direct the minds that will direct the world. Your sons are set apart to lead men to pure thoughts, lead them from temptations from the lower self and make them conscious of the self that lives with the Christ of God. In preparation, your sons will walk on many thorns. They will be faced with temptation like all other men. They will know the pain of hunger and of thirst; they will be mocked and imprisoned without cause. Many countries they will travel and at the feet of many masters they will sit, for they must learn like other men. Now it is time for you to go on your separate ways so they may begin their journey of life."

Elizabeth traveled by sea to rest in Jerusalem. She spent her time with John teaching all she had learned from the master. In the hills lived a man who was once a Rabi. He asked Elizabeth if John would accompany him to the great feast of Jerusalem. He taught John about the service of the Jews and the meaning of their sacrifices and their rituals. John witnessed the sacrificing of animals and could not understand how one's sin could be forgiven by the killing of these animals.

The Rabbi said to John, "God of heaven and earth does not require sacrificing. This cruel ceremony was borrowed from the idol worshippers of other lands. No sins were ever forgiven by sacrifice. In order for one to have his sins forgiven, one must return and purify their heart by love and righteousness, and then one shall be forgiven. It is a paying of debt. A man who has wronged another man cannot be forgiven unless the wrong is made right. Only the ones who do the wrong can make it right.

"The prophets look to you and say, 'He is Elijah!' (Translated as 'The Lord is God'). Elijah will come before the Messiah to pave his way and make the people ready to receive their king. Men comprehend the inner life by what they see and do; they come to God in ceremonies. John, you will make men know that sins may be washed away by the purity of life. In water, wash the bodies of people who would turn away sin and strive for purity. This is the rite of cleansing, those who are cleansed shall become the sons of purity and they shall be forgiven. This is the path you must follow, for you, John, are of purity."

Joseph and Mary went by the way of Jordan until they reached Nazareth, where Jesus grew up in Galilee. As a child, Jesus met many masters of Jewish faith and became a student and teacher of God's laws. The time came for Jesus to leave his mother and to travel the country, so he told her that he must travel beyond this land to see all of his Father's land. *I will meet with people who are not of Jewish faith, for all of the people are children of my Father God.*"

When Jesus left the temple walls, He saw multitudes of people of different races and colors. The people came to Jesus to hear His words. Jesus told the people that in God's eyes, every man is equal. *My Father is the one God who was, who is, and who shall be, who holds the scale of justice, whose boundless love has created all men to be equal; all men, whether they are white, black, red or yellow, can look upon His face and say our Father God.*"

Jesus taught that there is only one God and that our Father God is known as the Universal God. *All people worship God the One, but not all people see Him alike. In Egypt, he is Thoth, in Greece, he is Zeus, and Jehovah is his Jewish name. Everywhere there is root, from which things grow. You must not be afraid of God and do not treat him as a foe. You need no man, no priest to talk with God. You must not worship idols and sacrifice to please God. Give your life in service for the soul and God will be pleased.*

"The universal God is one, yet he is more then one. All things are God, all things are one. The flowers and the birds and beasts are all of God. Every fiber of every living thing is God. The God I speak of is everywhere, He is not just in a temple, and He has no bounds of any kind. The universal God is of wisdom and love. God's kingdom is not far away, it is not in the stars, it is not a country where we must go; it is a state of mind. Men with mortal eyes cannot see the kingdom of heaven, because it is within them. God never made a heaven or hell for man. We are the creator of our own heaven. Now cease to look for the heaven in the sky, open your heart and know what is inside. It is a flood of light, of boundless joy; this heaven is the kingdom you search for. To enter into this kingdom of God's, you must shed the lower self. In spirit form, one can enter the kingdom of heaven."

Even men who were known as thieves and extortionists sought to find the man called Jesus and to learn of God's laws. A man in the group spoke out to Jesus. "This will be an evil day for you, my Lord, for you are seen amongst the likes of us." And Jesus replied, *"A master will never hide himself from those who seek him. Men will judge other men for what they are, and not what they seem to be. These people who have sin are still children of my Father God. Their souls are just as precious in His sight as are those of the righteous. We are all a part of a brotherhood of all men."*

Jesus traveled the countryside from Persia to Babylon, Greece and Egypt. As he traveled, he taught and healed the sick. Returning from Egypt to his homeland of Galilee, he traveled to the Jordan River to find John the Harbinger. Jesus approached John, who was in the river purifying the souls of men, and shouted to the crowds, *"Behold, the man of God! Behold the greatest of seers! Behold! Elijah has returned!"*

John saw the multitude of people who followed Jesus and knew He was the King of Peace. "Behold!" shouted John. "Behold the King who comes in the name of God!"

Jesus put his hands on John's shoulders, smiled, and said, *"I would be washed in water as a symbol of cleansing of the soul."*

John replied, "You do not need to be washed, for you are one who is pure in thoughts and deeds. I am not worthy to perform this rite."

And Jesus said to John, *"I come as a model for all sons of man to follow. If man is to follow in my steps, then I must walk in theirs. As I bid men to do, then I must do also. All men must be washed, for this is a symbolic way of cleansing the soul. This washing we establish as a rite, a baptismal rite. You, John, must wash the multitude in the name of Christ. This is done to blot out sin. But first you must baptize me in the name of Christ."*

As John was baptizing Jesus, a dove flew down from the sky and landed on Jesus' head. The Archangel Gabriel looked down from the heavens and proclaimed,

"This is the well-beloved Son of God, the Christ.
He is the love of God in the form of man."

Then Jesus shouted out to the multitude of people who witnessed the voice from the heavens: *"You men of Israel, hear! The Kingdom is at hand. Behold the great key-keeper stands before you, along with the spirit of Elijah. Behold! When the key is turned, the mighty gates will open and all may greet the King. Behold! Indeed, the King has come. But do not look upon me as your King. Yes, your kingdom truly is at hand; but men cannot see it with carnal eyes, for this is the kingdom for the soul. Our Father God is this Kingdom. Men must not fear this messenger whom God sends forth. I am not sent to sit upon a throne to rule upon earthly possessions. I am not to rule as Caesar or to have claimant for the Jewish throne.*

"Men call me Christ, but Christ is not a man. The Christ is universal Love, and Love is King. Look not unto your flesh, for it is not king. Look to the Christ that is within, who shall be formed in every one of you as it has been formed in me. When you have purified your thoughts and deeds, this will cleanse the temple of the flesh. When you have purified your hearts by faith, the King will enter in. Do unto other men what you would have them do to you. Every soul is a kingdom; there is a king for every man. This is the kingdom of love, and love is the greatest power in life. It is the Christ, so Christ is King.

"Everyone may have this Christ dwell in his soul as the Christ dwells in my soul. The body is the temple of the king. As a man of God, I see with the eyes of the soul. When the son of man rises to the plane of the Christ Consciousness, he will know that he himself is also King. For the king is love and the love is Christ, all of you sons of man, prepare to meet your King."

As time passed for Jesus, living as a mortal man made him grow weary. His mind needed to be empty of negative thoughts; therefore, he entered the wilderness alone to consult with his Father. As he talked within Himself, he told His Father that his lower self was strong; there were many ties that bound him to the carnal ways of life. He wondered, 'Do I have the strength and the willingness to stand before the face of man? And when they demand proof that I am the Messiah, what will I say?'

Then came an unfamiliar voice from the stillness of the night that tried to tempt Jesus in the ways of carnal life. *"If you were to go into Jerusalem and from a temple pinnacle, cast down yourself to the earth, was it not written that He gives his angels to watch over you, and with their hands they will stand you up, so you would not dash your foot against earth or stone? Take that leap of faith and see if Your Father's hands will keep you!"*

Jesus said to the tempter *"It is written; do not put the Lord, your God, to the test!"* But the tempter tried again to seduce Jesus. *"Look forth upon the world; behold its honor and fame! Behold its wealth and pleasures! All of these I will give to you, if you worship me and not your Father."*

"Away with your tempting thoughts," yelled Jesus. *"My heart is fixed, for it is written, worship the Lord our God and serve only him! Now leave! Go back to the sinister place you slithered from. Your temptations are not welcome here, be gone!"*

During Jesus' travels, He would teach in parables to the crowds in order for them to retain His lessons. He would feed the multitudes of people who were hungry and heal the sick. He had the gift to make the blind see again. He would say to his people, *"As it was written by a prophet before my time, I will open my mouth to speak in parables; I will proclaim what has been hidden from the blinded eyes of the world."*

Even those who had doubted Jesus soon became believers. Jesus' own disciples were aboard a boat caught in a blinding storm, and as it was written in the bible, they witnessed as Jesus walked on water. The disciple Peter noticed a form shaped as a man moving on the waves. He yelled to the others, "Look! It is a ghost, a sign of evil things!" All the men were terrified and cried out in fear. A voice carried over the water towards the boat, *"Take heart, for it is I, do not be afraid,"* said the Lord.

Peter called out, "My Lord! My Lord! Can this be true?" Jesus reached forth his hands and said, "Come, step upon the waves." When Peter stepped out upon the water, it was as of solid rock. He walked on the waves - until the fear of sinking entered his mind! As quickly as Peter's thoughts were of falling into the water, they soon became reality; he fell deep into the sea. "Oh Lord, save me," cried Peter. Jesus took Peter by the hand, and guided him to the boat. *"Oh, you of little faith! Why did you doubt me?"*

Jesus performed many miracles. It was told of the case of Lazarus, whom Jesus had brought back from the dead. *"Behold! For Lazarus shall live again. I am the Resurrection and the Life; he who has faith in Me, though he is dead, yet shall he live; and who is alive, and has living faith in Me, shall never die."*

Many people who Jesus met on his journeys throughout the lands loved him. He also loved and cared for them no matter who they were or what they had done. On one of his travels, he came across a situation involving a woman whom the Pharisees had convicted as an adulterer. The man in charge of carrying out the sentence of stoning the woman to death approached Jesus and said, "This vile women has been taken in adultery and the laws state that such acts should result in being stoned to death." Jesus gazed into the women's eyes and felt her remorse.

"Who gives you the power to take a life? What sin has been committed that she should be put to death? Let him who has not sinned stand forth and be the first to stone her. Those who have not sinned would not take part in such ritual. I will stand by this woman and share in what punishment you pass"

Jesus closed his eyes and waited for the stoning to begin, but when He opened his eyes, the men who accused her were gone. The woman fell to the ground and begged for Jesus' forgiveness. He said, *"I condemn you not; go on your way and sin no more."*

News of Jesus spread throughout the lands like a swarm of locusts. He knew that He alone could not travel to many places, so he called upon His disciples. *"In the time of the great pharaohs of Egypt, my Father instilled the power unto Moses and Joshua to fend for the needs of the many. I, too, give the authority for you, my disciples, to go to the lost sheep of Israel to feed the hungry and cure every sickness.*

"Go and proclaim the good news that the kingdom of heaven has come near. Take no gold or silver in your belts, do this in love and honor for our Father. I'm sending sheep amongst wolves; be wise as the serpent and innocent as doves. If there is anyone who will not welcome you, shake off the dust from thy feet and leave them. You will be dragged before governors and kings because of me. Fear not what to say, for you will be given the words, the words of our Father, who shall speak through you. Go now and proclaim that the Kingdom of Heaven is near."

While Jesus was in distant lands in Jerusalem, the Pharisees were busy plotting a way to seize Jesus. They decided that this deed must be accomplished in a secret way. Jesus must be taken when the crowds were not near to prevent a riot or even a battle. It so happened that they heard that one of the twelve men who traveled with Jesus, Judas, worshiped wealth. For a sum of money this man might take them to the place where Jesus would be alone. So they found Judas, called him aside and told him that the rulers and high priests of Jerusalem would consult with Jesus. "They would know of His claims and if He proves to be the Messiah, they will stand in His defense," they told Judas. "This must be done in private, away from the crowds and His disciples. If you will lead the priests to your master, we will pay a sum of silver to you."

Judas reasoned with himself that it surely might be well to give the Lord a chance to tell the priest of His claims. If they tried to do Him harm, He had the power to disappear, as He had done before. Thirty pieces of silver was a wealthy sum and it could be used for food and shelter on their journey. "Yes!" cried Judas, "I will lead the way. Let it be known and make no mistake, a kiss will reveal to you the Lord."

The following evening, Jesus sat with his disciples, with Mary of Magdalene by his side, for the feast. He smiled at the woman as he touched her hand and said, *"Behold the lesson of the hour. This is the hour I truly praise the name of God, for this will be the last time I will feast with you all. When we feast again, it will be in my father's kingdom. Truly I tell you, one of you will betray me."*

The disciples became greatly distressed and began to say, one after the other, "Surely not I, Lord!" Peter asked of Mary, who was seated by the Lord, "To whom does he refer? Which one of us is so depraved as to betray his Lord?" *"Look upon this dish I hold and see who shares with me this last morsel,"* said the Lord. They looked as Judas pulled his hand away from the dish and Jesus said to Judas, *"The Prophets cannot fail; the son of man must be betrayed, woe to him who shall betray the Lord, do quickly what you must do."*

Judas pushed his way to the door. "This must not happen, my Lord. By my sword, I vow that no one shall harm you," exclaimed Peter. "Yes, my Lord," cried Mary, "We will leave this place and hide; no harm will come to you if you are gone."

"It is written, the way of my demise," said Jesus. *"Let us rejoice, for I will be in My Father's Kingdom. Let us share this loaf of bread. See the bread as a symbol of my body and see it as a symbol of life. As I take this loaf and break it, so shall my flesh be broken so men will see the sacrifice I gave for all men to be free. So eat this bread of everlasting life and remember me.*

"As you drink this wine, you shall drink in faith. The wine is the blood-line of the grape as the blood of man is the blood-line of carnal self. The wine is a symbol of life. You shall drink this wine, and keep it pure as if it were the Christ. And may the bloodlines of all men be as absolute as the Son of Man. This is the feast of life, our last supper. This day will be remembered and henceforth, this bread and wine shall be the remembrance of me. So drink this wine, eat this bread, and remember me. I give you a new commandment to learn. As I love you and give my life for you, so shall you love the world and give your life to save her. Love one another as you love yourself, and then the world will know that you are sons of God, disciples of the Son of Man God has glorified.

"All of you will become deserters because of me, tonight," said Jesus. *"Only you, Mary, would stand by my side, but I forbid you to do so, for you would be harmed. Go to my Mother's haven and stay until the time of reckoning has passed."*

Peter boasted, "I would lay down my life for you! I will never desert you, my Lord." Then Jesus said to Peter, *"Boast not of your bravery, my friend, you are not strong enough to follow me tonight. Truly, I tell you, this very night, before the cock crows, you will deny me three times. All of you will estrange from me tonight. Let not your heart be sad; you all believe in God; believe in me. Behold, there are many mansions in my Father's Kingdom. I will go unto my Father's land and prepare a place for you.*

"I am the way, the truth of life; I manifest the Christ in God. No one comes unto the Father, but through who I Am. The Christ is Light, the Christ is Love. These are the words and works of God, who lives in me as I live in Him."

"The hour has come when you will weep; and the wicked will rejoice, because I will go away. But I will rise and your sorrows shall turn to joy. You will rejoice as one welcomes his brothers back from the dead. It is time for you to scatter. The wicked men soon will be here. I will not be alone, for my Father is here with me. Go now, for its time to be judged by your peers."

It came to pass that Judas arrived at the garden where Jesus had stayed to pray. The head priest and a crowd of people carrying swords had accompanied Judas to find Jesus. Judas had told them what his signal would be: "The one I kiss will be Jesus." Judas approached Jesus and said, "My Lord, what have I done? You are given powers to disappear from this unruly crowd, and why won't you do so?" As Judas kissed Him, Jesus said to Judas, *"Friend, do what you have to do, for it is proclaimed that you place upon my head the kiss of death. Do so, and go on with your affairs."*

The crowds laid hold of Jesus and bound him in ropes. Jesus asked his accusers, *"Why do you come in the dead of the night with swords and clubs to take me from this sacred place? Have I not spoken in a public place in Jerusalem? You could have found me on any day."*

Suddenly Peter appeared; he had come to try and save the Lord. He drew his sword and wounded one of the Priests. *"Put away your sword!"* cried Jesus. *"For all who take the sword will perish by the sword. Do you think that I cannot appeal to My Father and He would send legions of angels to my side? All this must take place so that the scriptures of the prophets may be fulfilled. Go now, my friend, and let me be trialed alone."* Jesus approached the wounded priest and laid His hands on his wound. *"Please forgive Peter for what he has done. The love of my Father will heal you. Go now, for you are healed."* The priest was, indeed, healed and was astonished by the miracle Jesus had performed, but the head priest called it blasphemy, for no man has the supremacy to do this deed.

Those who had arrested Jesus took him to Caiaphas, the Jewish high priest. In the distance, hiding from the crowd, Peter was watching to see if they would harm the Lord. The council gathered and was looking for testimony against Jesus so they could put him to death. Many false witnesses came forward, but there was no proof of blasphemy.

As Peter was sitting outside of the courtyard trying to catch sight of what was happening; a servant girl came to Peter and said to him, "You also were with Jesus the Galilean."

However, Peter denied that he knew Jesus and went another way. Again, another girl said to a bystander, "This man was with Jesus of Nazareth!" And again, Peter denied he knew of him.

Finally, yet another bystander approached Peter and said, "Certainly you are one of them who follow Jesus, for your accent betrays you." Now Peter began to curse and he swore an oath. "I do not know this man!" At that moment, the cock crowed and Peter remembered what Jesus had said to him, that before the cock crowed, he would deny his Lord three times. Peter ran into the wilderness, ashamed of what he had done.

At first morning light, the priests concurred that Jesus must be put to death. They bound Him and led Him away to the governor, Pontius Pilate. Pilate asked the Jews, "What was the commotion here this morning?" They responded, "We bring you an evil and seditious man. He has been put on trial before the highest council of Jews, for he is proven a traitor. We pray that you put this blasphemer to death!"

"Why do you bring him to me?" asked Pilate. "Go and judge this man yourselves. You have your own Jewish laws and according to the Roman laws, you have the right to judge and execute,"

"We have no right to execute this man," said Pilate. "According to Roman law, no man should be found guilty of a crime until all of the testimony is in and the accused is permitted to defend himself."

But the accusers of Jesus persisted; "We charge that Jesus is an enemy of Rome; He claims that He should be King,"

Pilate approached Jesus and asked, "What are your answers to these charges? Are they true or false? Is it true that you claim to be a king?"

Jesus answered, ***"Why should I plead before the carnal courts? These charges were brought up by perjured men. Yes, I am King, but carnal eyes cannot see the kingdom of God, for it is within. If I were a King as*** *carnal Kings, I would have my armies stand in my defense. I would not surrender to the minions of the Jewish laws. I have no testimony, God is my Witness, and my words and deeds bear witness to the Truth. Every man who comprehends the Truth will listen to My words, and their souls will give witness unto me, this is the Truth that I know."*

"This man is not guilty of any crime," said Pilate. "I cannot sentence this man to death."

"But he must be crucified!" cried the Jews. *"This man would falsify a nation of Jews!"*

Pilate pleaded with the crowd, "There are three men who are sentenced to be crucified. These men are murderers. According to your Jewish custom, at the end of every year, you will heap all of your sins upon the head of someone. This man would become the scapegoat for all of your sins. When you send this man out into the wilderness, then you are released from sin. According to your custom, today I will release to you the prisoner Barabbas, who has been sentenced for murder. Now hear me! I plead that you let Jesus be released and let Barabbas serve his debt on the cross. Send Jesus out into the wilderness and hear of him no more!" The crowd was enraged to hear what Pilate said; they began a plot to tear apart the Roman palace and to drive Pilate away.

Pilate's wife, who had the gift of prophecy, said to Pilate, *"Beware of what you do this hour, do not touch this man from Galilee, for He is a holy man indeed. I have seen Him walk on water and raise the dead. I saw Jerusalem covered in blood, and a veil covering the sun. The earth on which I stood was shaken and the day turned into night. I tell you, my husband; do not bathe your hands in this man's blood. If you hurt this man, you hurt the Son of God."*

Pilate turned to the crowd and spoke. "This man, whom you have accused, is the Son of the Most Holy God! I proclaim my innocence! If you would shed His blood, His blood will be on your hands, not mine. I take this water and wash my hands from this wrongdoing. You are fools to be so blinded! This is your King, the King you have been waiting for, the Messiah that you will put to death!" Pilate instructed his soldiers not to harm Jesus, but to return Him to the Jews. His blood would not be on Roman hands.

"What are we to do?" said the leader of the Jews. "It is against our laws to crucify any man, but it is permitted in our laws to stone him to death." So the mob cried out, "Let Him be stoned!" And they dragged Jesus toward the place for stoning.

Along the way, a group of Roman soldiers belonging to King Herod approached the mob. A Pharisee called out to the Romans, "This Man is a traitor! He claims that He should be King. Surely you would crucify the Man." Now these guards, who would have no remorse and would instead find joy in crucifying Jews, quickly agreed. They ordered the mob to have Jesus bear the cross to the place of the crucifixion. The mob took up the cry, "Let Him be crucified!"

Jesus trudged the road to Calvary, struggling with the cross while the mob stoned and beat Him. On the way, a man by the name of Simon, a friend of Jesus, ran up to the Lord and said, "My Lord, why do they wish to harm you? You are a gentle man, a Man of Peace!" Unable to answer, Jesus fell to the ground out of pure exhaustion. The Romans yelled to Jesus, "Rise, or die in the spot where you lay!" Simon called out, "Let me help this man, for He has no strength in Him to bear this cross! I will bear this cross for Him." And so he did. Simon hoisted the cross on his shoulder and dragged it all the way to Calvary.

Among the crowd, Judas awaited for the Lord to assert His powers and demonstrate the power of God. When he saw his Master lying on the ground covered in blood he said to himself, "O Lord, what have I done? I have betrayed the Son of God." Judas ran from the place where Jesus was tormented and went to the temple where he had been compensated the sum of silver for betraying the Lord. Take back your bribe!" cried Judas. "I have betrayed the Son of God." He threw the silver on the floor and climbed the temple walls. From there he tied a rope around his neck and made his last request. "Please, my Lord, forgive me. I know I will never be permitted to enter your Father's Kingdom, so I will go now to the place known for suffering." And Judas hung himself from the perch of the temple walls.

The mob pushed on to Calvary, as the Roman soldiers had already bound the two other prisoners to the cross. Four other soldiers were appointed to put Jesus to death. These are the men who put the crown of thorns upon his head and mocked him for his claims that he was King. Instead of using cord to bind Jesus to the cross, they drove nails through His feet and hands and erected the cross between the other two crosses. When finished, they sat down with the mob to watch Jesus die.

Jesus looked into the heavens and beseeched His Father, *"Father, please forgive them, for they know not what they do!"*

To the crowd he proclaimed, *"I will die for all sins on earth to be forgiven. Please remember me as a channel of love for our Father God. Remember me as a deliverer of goodness; do not remember me suffering on this cross. I will return again after my death. I will return in spirit, one of light bodies, not of flesh. Then you will witness the promise; the promise of everlasting life given by God, the promise that your soul will live forever with the Father."*

The Jewish crowd was wild, calling out, "Behold our false King, who claims to be our Messiah! If you are truly the Son of God, break free from the cross and save yourself." Even the Romans joined in the mockery, "Our allegiance is with Caesar! He is Our King! All hail, Caesar, the true King of the Roman empire!"

News came to Pilate that Jesus was to be crucified by King Herod's men. Out of anger, he commissioned a tablet to be placed upon the cross. He then dispatched his fastest riders to deliver and place the tablet on the cross with these words of truth:

"Jesus the Christ, King of the Jews." The priests were angered when they read these words and demanded them to be removed. The messenger read Pilate's order and it said, "What I have written, I have written, and let it stand. Today is the day you put your King to death."

One of the men tied to a cross next to Jesus also mocked Him. "If you are the Christ, you then have the power to send lightning bolts at these men. Why not save yourself and me?" The third man on the cross rebuked the man, saying, "Have you no fear in God? This Man has not committed any crimes. Why is he punished in the way of those who are murderers and thieves? We are condemned to die today for the crimes we have inflicted onto others, for this is the debt we owe. But you, Lord, have never committed a crime. It is a wrongdoing, the pain and suffering they have inflicted on you. I have heard of your teachings, is it true that our Kingdom comes? Will our sins be forgiven? Will there be a place in your Father's Kingdom for me?"

And Jesus said, *"Behold, I will meet you today in the Kingdom of souls. I am the way of the light into my Father's Kingdom. Today I shall sacrifice so that all men will be forgiven."*

Jesus' mother Mary, his brother James, and Mary of Magdalene stood at the foot of the cross, steadfast among the unruly crowd. "My beloved son, why do they do this to you? This is injustice they have done to you. You shall all go to purgatory for what you have done to my son," cried Mary, as her son James tried to comfort her. Mary of Magdalene wept at the sight of her Lord, for she loved him as a wife would love a husband. Mary said, "You have prepared me for this day, my Lord, and yet I'm not prepared for what I have witnessed today. Why must you suffer this way? Why do you give in to the damned? Does not your Father frown on those who take contentment hurting His beloved son? Why does He not cast down His wrath and smite these wrongdoers?"

Jesus said to both Marys, *"It is ordained that it shall happen this way, for this will be the day that I will be remembered. Also, it will be known when I will rise again. Look for me on the third day and you will see how it is to be of one soul, free from all carnal bondage."*

The day turned into night, though the sun had been up for only a few hours. "What witchery is this?" cried the mob. They built large fires so they could see the Lord suffer on the cross. The sun refused to shine all day and the Lord yelled out, "*My Father! Have you forsaken me? Why does the sun cease to shine?*" The hours passed, and then, in the darkness of the sunless day, the earth began to shake.

Finally, a flood of golden light appeared above Jesus' head. Jesus lifted up His head toward the heavens and said, "*Father, I give you my soul.*" The earth began to rumble more intensely and the rocks split in two as the earth opened. Tombs rose from the ground; some thought they saw the dead walk the streets. A soldier who had kept watch over Jesus during the crucifixion exclaimed, "This man was truly the Son of God!"

When evening came, the lifeless body of Jesus was still nailed to the cross. Mary pleaded for the soldiers to free her son. A man by the name of Joseph of Arimathea approached the guards and said, "By the permission of Pilate, my job is to prepare the body for entombment." Mary recognized Joseph as a friend and a great admirer of Jesus; a man that was known for his generosity. He would have been known as one of the disciples, but his life with his family kept him close to his place of origin. Nevertheless, when Jesus visited Jerusalem, Joseph's home had always been a haven for Jesus and his flock.

Joseph held Mary and wept with her. "What have they done to my brother and loyal friend? These men will be judged for the crimes they have inflicted upon the Lord this day; they will be shown no mercy on their souls when they convene with God." Joseph lowered Jesus down from the cross and laid him in his mother's lap.

Mary of Magdalene washed the dried blood from Jesus' weathered face, hands and feet. "I shall never forget you, my Lord," said Mary of Magdalene. "You will always be with me in flesh and spirit. The bloodline of your truth is within me and will multiply in the passing of time." Joseph wrapped Jesus' body in clean linen cloths and brought Him to the tomb made personally for Joseph, for his time of death. With deep sorrow, Joseph sighed, "My Lord, I give to you my final resting place. May you find peace and rest. One day we will meet at your peaceful dwelling. You will welcome me as I have welcomed you into my heart. I shall leave and enclose you in this tomb so no one will devastate this sacred place."

Outside of the tomb, Joseph sought the help of over twenty men to roll a large stone to cover the entrance of the tomb. "No one may enter this place," said Joseph. "This is the final resting place of our Lord. May He find peace and love in His Father's Kingdom and forget the pain and suffering that men have bestowed upon him."

The priest who was responsible for crucifying Jesus was fearful that friends of Jesus would rob the body from the tomb. He feared that if the people thought that that the rumor was true that the Nazarene had risen from the dead, it would abolish the foundations of all Jewish beliefs that the Messiah is still yet to come. The priest asked Pilate if he would order the Roman soldiers to guard the tomb. Pilate replied, "The Jews have soldiers, so use your own soldiers to guard the tomb. I have washed my hands from this immoral deed you have done. You now must bear all of the responsibility."

So the Jewish soldiers were ordered to guard the tomb, but first, the priests wanted to make sure that the man from Nazarene was still in the tomb. The soldiers rolled the rock from the entrance of the tomb and four priests entered. Frightening thoughts entered their minds while they were making their way to the back of the tomb. 'If this man has risen, he may be waiting in the shadows to have revenge for what was inflicted on him,' thought one priest. 'If he returned as a ghost, will we be haunted to our deaths?' thought another.

Finally, when they arrived at the spot where Jesus lay, one of the priests thought he saw the man of Nazareth walking in the room. He ran outside of the tomb in fear, running toward the soldiers and crying, "It's true, it's true, He has risen!" But quickly following him came the other priests, denying that Jesus had risen. One said, "He is wrapped in cloth, as His body lays lifeless on the stone. We will seal this cave and guard it so that no one will steal His body from this tomb." Two days passed and everything was quiet. The priests watched the tomb with the soldiers; they were convinced that the Nazarene's followers had abandoned the thoughts of stealing the body. They had the guards swear an oath to guard this tomb with their lives. Also, for his allegiance, each man was paid an extra sum of silver.

On the third night, just past midnight, a blaze of light descending from the heavens awakened the soldiers. The light encircled the tomb and the ground began to shake as it had done on the day Jesus was put to death. Ghostly figures appeared around the tomb, as the stone was rolled from the entrance. A voice from the heavens called out, *The man who once was Jesus is no longer here. He has risen as The Christ. The light of Christ surrounds you. Henceforth, here is the good news; The Christ has risen! He is now seated in his Fathers Kingdom, the Kingdom of Heaven.*

The Guards were terrified. Running outside in fear, they reported back to the priests, "He has risen!" they cried. "The stone no longer blocks the tomb entrance. It was a legion of angels that has set him free. I tell you, He is truly the Son of God!"

The priests reminded the soldiers of their oath. "No one is to know what has happened tonight. Since the body is nowhere to be found, you must say that someone has stolen the body from the tomb. Go now, and hold your tongues, for this will never be spoken of again. If this news were to go forth that Jesus has risen, all men would believe he is the Son of God." The priests made an oath to keep quiet about what had happened.

The next morning, both Marys visited the tomb to pay their respects. To their surprise, they found the large stone rolled away from the entrance tomb. "Someone has desecrated my Son's tomb," said Mary as she ran inside. When she arrived at the place where Jesus had been laid, she noticed that the cloth he had worn was folded neatly in a pile. She cried out to Mary of Magdalene, "What barbaric being has stolen my Son's body?" Out of the shadows, the silhouette of a man appeared and Mary called to him, "Was it you who took my Son?"

Mary heard the man say, *"Behold! My Mother - I told you that I would meet you at this tomb, on this day."*

Mary of Magdalene approached the figure and fell to her knees with disbelief. "My Lord! Say it is true that you have come back from the dead."

Jesus said to both Marys, *"Do not look for the living among the dead, and do not look for me in the flesh. I have risen! My soul and carnal self is of one soul. There will not be any remains of the flesh body to be found. This is what I tell you, to be one as the Father. Go, now, and find the others, so they will witness the One who is risen."*

Mary of Magdalene went forth, found Peter, and told him of the blessed event. Peter gathered the disciples and went to Galilee to the mountain to which Jesus had directed them to go upon word of his resurrection. The doubting Thomas was not convinced that the Lord had risen. "We have seen with our own eyes the passing of our Lord," said Thomas. A voice from the shadows answered, *"Why do you doubt when you never have doubted before? Haven't I been truthful? Yes, Thomas! I have risen!"*

Jesus welcomed his disciples and gave them their last duty. *"All authority of heaven and earth has been given to me. Go therefore and make disciples of all nations. Teach them everything I have taught you. Baptize in the name of the Father, the Son, and the Holy Spirit and remember that I am with you always, to the end of the Age."*

The New Age

Chapter Seventeen

Life is just a performance. Good day to you, it is I, Indigo. Yes, we see you have heard that cliché before. The life you live on earth is what we call 'the play of life'. You see, dear ones, before you chose to live life on earth, you determined what type of life would benefit your spiritual growth. You are the writer and the creator of your very own destiny. So one may ask, why am I not a millionaire, or why do I have a deadly disease or deformity, and why is life so hard? Why not just make life easy?

In the beginning, your soul is a vibration of devotion and privilege. You are a form of God that is created in his own image. To be ascended is to be honored. And how is one to grow spiritually when one's true 'being-ness' is already pure? This is when your being-ness is split into many; it is divided into many lower beings while still connected unto the true self of the one. This happens so that you may live as an un-ascended being, experiencing adversity, sorrow, misery, devotion, tranquility and contentment.

The reality of your being-ness that resides on earth is of subordinate vibrations to the ones who are ascended onto the higher realms of existence. We do feel the anguish of your realm through Joseph and are remorseful for the endurance one must go through for one's growth. The way you live your existence is the path you have chosen for your own personal growth. The more difficult the obstacles in your path, the more enlightened with growth you become.

For many years the beings of earth have lived without harmony, enduring the invading and killing of others for prejudicial reasons. This has resulted in a waste of life, all for wealth and power. There must be an end to this ego, for it is destroying the true essence of your being-ness and what surrounds you. The dawn of the age of Pisces began when Jesus entered your earthly realm over two thousand years ago. Jesus promised at the end of this age that he would return to earth at the dawn of the New Age of Aquarius to fulfill the prophecy that our souls would live forever and reside in the Father's Kingdom from now until eternity.

What's an Age?

One might ask what an Age is. It takes the Earth and its neighboring planets twenty-six thousand years to rotate around the ecliptic; this orbit is called the Astrological Zodiac. The Astrological Zodiac is divided into twelve signs. See below:

Astrological Signs the twelve signing in the Zodiac calendar. ♒ Aquarius (Water Bearer): Jan. 20–Feb 18 ♓ Pisces (Fish): Feb. 19–March 20 ♈ Aries (Ram): March 21–April 19 ♉ Taurus (Bull): April 20–May 20 ♊ Gemini (Twins): May 21–June 20 ♋ Cancer (Crab): June 21–July 22 ♌ Leo (Lion): July 23–Aug. 22 ♍ Virgo (Virgin): Aug. 23–Sept. 22 ♎ Libra (Scales): Sept. 23–Oct. 22 ♏ Scorpio (Scorpion): Oct. 23–Nov. 21 ♐ Sagittarius (Archer): Nov. 22–Dec. 21 ♑ Capricorn (Goat): Dec. 22–Jan. 19

It takes your solar system around 2100 years to pass through one of these signs; this is known as an Astrological Age. When time passes through one sign and into the next new sign, it becomes a New Age. The end is near for the age of Pisces and we will welcome in the New Age of Aquarius.

When a full cycle of all twelve signs is completed, this is what is called a Cosmic Year, or Yuga. It takes about 26,000 years for the earth to rotate through all of the signs. The Earth is now entering into a new Cosmic Year as well as a New Astrological Age; the Age of Aquarius. When a new Cosmic Year begins, it is referred to as the Golden Years. This New Age will be called the Golden Years because you are now at the beginning of another new cycle.

These cycles are named after the earth's metals and are related to the spiritual awareness of beings. In the beginning, when the earth first came into manifestation, the first Yuga began. It is known as the **Satya Yuga,** meaning purity; symbolized by gold, it became the Golden Age. Humanity at that time was barely removed from its godlike innocence. This is when one's self was whole, a mirror of God.

When time passed, around sixty five hundred years or so, you moved into the **Age of Tetra,** the Silver Age. Spiritual awareness had decreased and some men had parted from God. Materialism was important to some. A few spiritual minds became lost and the physical reality became real. When the **Dvapara Yuga,** or the Copper Age arrived, negativity had hold on humanity's awareness. The earth entered into a dark time known as the "Dark Ages." The Light of God was divided among man and darkness grew as time passed.

Currently the earth is in the **Kali Yuga,** or the Iron Age, which is known as the dregs of time, and began in 3102 B.C. Around ninety percent of humanity had turned from the light. God did send messengers of hope for man to follow; he gave man Moses, Joshua, and Jesus, to name a few. These great men brought light into the eyes of man. Humanity has accepted the teaching of these great messengers of God, and is ready to move into the next stage of life destined to occur at the Grand Conjunction.

The Grand Conjunction is the alignment of all three ages; the New Age of Aquarius, the new Cosmic Year, and the Golden Age. The conversion of all three ages will take place in the near future, making human beings Godlike once more. One might wonder if this is the first Grand Conjunction of the Ages. There is no documentation on such a grand event, but being that the earth is over 4.5 billion years old, the conditions have occurred before.

There is evidence that an advanced civilization might have lived upon, or visited, the Earth before. However, there is lack of absolute proof. Consider the pyramids in Egypt. The temple standing near the Great Sphinx in Giza was built of limestone blocks, each weighing over four thousand pounds. These blocks were raised and stacked over four hundred feet above the desert floor and leveled perfectly. It is one of the tallest structures on earth. In fact, three football fields can be housed in one of these pyramids. The hallways leading to the chambers in this great pyramid look as if they were sliced with a fine cutting tool, just like a hot knife would slice through butter. These structures were built over forty five hundred years ago. The Egyptians were a unique race, but were the pyramids built at the time of the first Pharaoh? Or did the Egyptians of 3100 BC and beyond inherit these structures from visitors who were more advanced than humanity in their time?

These visitors may have brought the knowledge of their heritage and left an indication of who they were. The Egyptians adopted their ways and worshipped them as gods. When the visitors returned to their place of origin, they left behind monuments of what had served to remind them of their own home world. The Egyptians held the memories of the visitors as gods for many dynasties. It was not until the time of Ramses II of the nineteenth dynasty that the Egyptians began to doubt their gods. This was when the one and only true God appointed Moses to free the Jews from bondage.

Peru also shows evidence of an ancient civilization left in ruins. Regarding the mysterious Peruvian Pyramids, where are the Incas who built them? Can a civilization just disappear from the face of the earth?

Also, there are drawings that were created by the Nazca culture between 200 BC and 600 AD known as the Nazca lines; they can only be seen at a high altitude. These lines were made by removing the iron-oxide coated pebbles which cover the surface of the Nazca desert. When the gravel is removed, they contrast with the light-colored earth underneath. There are several hundred simple lines and geometric patterns on the Nazca plateau, as well as over seventy animal, insect, and human figures of curvilinear design. One even resembles what some might call an 'astronaut'. The area encompassing the lines is nearly 200 square miles, and the largest figures are nearly 900 feet long. Was this a welcome sign for traveling visitors? Why else would anyone build such an enormous greeting that could only be seen from the heavens?

One may ask, "If the earth is billions of years old, why isn't there any evidence of life before the prehistoric age?" The earth grows in a cycle, and when the earth is unbalanced, she purges herself by shifting the landmasses around. This is when the land sinks into the ocean, hiding the old world, while the ocean floor surfaces to create new landmasses. In the New Age, the earth herself will be moving into a higher vibration, which will become utopia for all of mankind. All living things on earth will go through an evolution and the human D.N.A. will change. Once your being-ness is godlike, it is time for humanity to return to its original form of energy; it is time to come home.

The word "energy" is a powerful word and it is not the energy that you are accustomed to; it is the universal life force. The Christ is of this energy and through him, all things were made. Imagine your being-ness not of the flesh, but of pure energy and your thoughts made into reality. You can choose your appearance and your surroundings and food is no longer needed for nourishment. Disease, deformities and death will no longer exist, for this is the time of "no ego".

Since you will be of pure energy, filled with love and happiness, the importance in life is the goodness you bring to others. Yes, dear ones, this is the time we have been preparing you for, the merging of your higher self with your lower self. You are now one, you are now Self. Yes, the earth will soon be heaven, but before the earth becomes a paradise, all things on earth will go through a transformation. This event will take place for your spiritual growth. What might seem like the end is really a beautiful beginning.

A Message from Sparrow Hawk

Welcome - I Am Sparrow Hawk, the Protector of Mother Earth. The time for change is near! The earth will cry no more, for she will connect to the universe and reunite with her family once more. The earth has always kept her balance until the past century. The occupiers of the earth have ravaged her. The once blue beacon in space is not as pure as she was. The Earth is sick! It is time for the earth to help herself to become the planet she once was. She has begun her transition with climate changes, unusual weather, storms, earthquakes and floods, and this condition will worsen before it can get better.

When she is ready, the earth will turn on her side and begin to rotate in the opposite direction, which will cause chaos and destruction for her inhabitants. Large landmasses will sink into the ocean to be covered for an eternity, and new landmasses will surface clean and pure. Some animals will escape the wrath of God and populate the new landmasses, only to evolve into new species of light.

A Message from Patrick

Greetings, it is Patrick. We are so sorry! We hope that Sparrow Hawk did not scare you. Before the change comes, many will perish and life as you know it will no longer exist. You will feel as if God is punishing you. Remember, God loves you. What might seem like the end of all things is really the beginning. Many people will survive the transition and those beings that survive the shift chose to be on earth at this time for this reason. The human D.N.A. will change during the transition.

Soon all eyes will open to what the universe has in store for them and they will change into pure light. Masters and Teachers will pave the way for all to follow the new way of life. The non-survivors will understand what occurred when they arrive in the astral plane. They will witness the ascension of all mankind and of the earth onto a higher plane of enlightenment. The earth will now be a part of heaven. All beings will be of pure light; there will be no physical entities. The entire departed of the astral plane now will be able to visit and live on the earth. They will be reunited with loved ones to share an eternity together, and the earth will now be fifth-dimensional. What seems like the end of the world is really the beginning of a beautiful new world.

Take care, dear ones - The Collective.

Different Faces and Places

Chapter Eighteen

Have you ever wondered if there is life elsewhere other than on Earth? Are those unidentified flying objects (UFOS) that people claim to see real or hoaxes? In Peru, the ancient ruins are very mysterious and some believe there is a powerful energy vortex connected to them. The patterns marked in the earth in Peru can only be seen by air. Most of the Peruvian people have had, or know of someone who has had, a UFO experience. Most Peruvians believe that UFOs are real and nothing extraordinary. Are there extraterrestrial beings that reside at different places in the universe, some even here on Earth? It is hard to believe we are the only life God created, since space seems to be infinite.

What about the Bejianes; who are they? Is there truth in Deborah's claim to having guides who are extraterrestrial and to her claim that Indigo is extraterrestrial? Are these beings a threat to the human race, or are they here to observe and to help? These are some of the questions that I had and that you may be asking yourself by now.

Indigo is truly a different energy. When I channel Indigo, observers can see a distinct change in my appearance. My face takes on a different shape and my smile becomes very big; it is as though my face is being increased somehow to accommodate the appearance of another being or species. My hand movements go inwards in a pattern that feels to me as though we are moving energy. As Indigo, I speak in a soft and gentle voice, moving my hands with the fingers held in the shape of a triangle. I asked Indigo, "Who are you? What is your purpose?" and also, "Is there life other than what we know on earth?" This is what he had to say:

Indigo on the Subject of Life on Other Planets

When the Creator created the earth, the plan was to have Earth resemble the universe. The lessons to be learned by the people of the earth were of peace, love and harmony among themselves. God intended for the earth to have diversification of heritages, cultures, and beliefs. God's lesson in life for humans was to learn to live in harmony with one another, looking beyond any differences. If the blending of the inhabitants worked, Earth would be ready to join the rest of the universe in having peace and harmony.

Information from beings of other worlds has been channeled to your planet since humanity has inhabited the earth. Also, beings have been traveling to other worlds throughout the universe since time began. Not all beings from other worlds are so different from you. The fiber of your being is similar to those that resided on the earth thousands of years in your past time. Your brothers reside as a higher vibration than earth. They are from parts of the universe you are not aware of. These humans we speak of are your ancestors. You are created in the same mold as God created them. The difference is that they are made up of a higher vibration than you are, and they are connected directly to the Universal Life Force, which is God.

In their existence there is no doubt; there is only truth in how they live their life. From their seed came the blueprint of the human race of today; this is the missing link, you might say. In the New Age, earth's vibration will once more be in harmony with your ancestors. This is the time when you will unite with your forefathers and will be able to communicate with them one to one. They will help to reshape the earth and its beings. They will educate you about other beings who reside in the universe. When visited by others who mirror the human race, you will feel less threatened, and in time, they will introduce you to a new race of beings that were created by God.

After uniting with your forefathers and working on the rebuilding of the earth, it will be time to meet others from worlds now a part of your vibration. This is when you will meet other beings of God like the Indigo species. We are one with the Light, meaning we are one with spirit; we are our *true selves*. Our species are the source of the Light, meaning we can project the Light of the creator to where it's needed, for we are created from pure Light. We are complete; our higher and lower selves are merged into one self. We are of the "Christ", meaning we are a part of the "Christ Consciousness". Our energies are of many colors. When you look into a prism of multiple colors, you would witness the true form of the Indigo species.

Before the Indigo species was of Light, we, too, dwelt at a lower vibration. It was a similar situation to that of the earth; we inhabited a physical body as you do. If you were to meet the Indigo species when we were physical, you would have to forget the science fiction creatures you may expect us to look like. In fact, we are a pleasant species and you might even use the word "cute" when describing us! When we were physical we had two arms, two legs, and two eyes with a nose and a mouth as humans have. We would stand around five feet tall with large heads, huge smiles, and voices filled with laughter.

This is how our species was before we evolved into beings of the Light. As beings of the Light, we have families like you and jobs to which we must attend. I, Indigo, am a healer and a teacher of God's laws. I use my gift of projection to inform those who are like Joseph so that he can teach others - like you - about the Creator. We may look different to you, but then again, you look different to us!

Please do not confuse us with the extraterrestrials called the Grays. These beings are not of the Light, but dwellers of darkness. They have small gray bodies that stand around four feet tall with large heads and black, almond-shaped eyes. They are responsible for many sightings of UFOS on your planet as well as much abduction of your loved ones and even the mutilation of animals. Again I say, these extraterrestrial beings are not from the Light. We regret to say that there is a dark side and earth is subject to its experimentation.

The Grays are more technologically advanced than the third-dimensional human race. They were the invaders of your home world. The Creator has forbidden them to return to Earth. Once they were a part of the Light, but now they exist in the darkness. They are very interested in the human race on Earth, for they cannot understand the feeling of one who is of Light. Humans who have been abducted by these beings seem to describe this same species as their abductors. The Grays have experimented on humans for thousands of years. Most early UFO sightings have been the Grays, since they are a third dimensional being, like inhabitants of the earth.

The Grays have produced a new race by breeding with human D.N.A. to create a being of half-light. These new beings are partially in tune with the Light because they are part human. The Grays cannot understand this new species because they do not understand the Light. The half-breeds are trying to reach out for the human race; they want to be saved from the dark side because they feel abandoned and alone. They do not understand the side of themselves that prefers to dwell in the dark; they want to be a part of the Light. When the time comes for your forefathers to return to earth, your half brothers will return to Earth as well. This new species will want love from humans, for this is what the Grays could not give to them.

Will the human race be ready for these refugees from the dark?
Will the human race be ready to meet earth's forefathers
when they return?

As the time comes near for the earth to change, there will be many UFO sightings of beings of Light. Strangers among you will purposely show themselves in order to make the people of the earth aware that there is, indeed, more to life than what we know; that life is out there. There will be extraterrestrials who will visit your earth, so please welcome them. They will be in human form and you will never know if you have met one or not. We are not invaders of your home world. Our purpose is to help the inhabitants of the earth to survive the coming changes and to teach of the new laws of the universe. We are known as "The Friendly."

Deborah helped us set up your matrix, Joseph. In other words, she helped us to lay a foundation to keep you balanced so that the collective would be able to transmit messages through you. She claimed that her channels were extraterrestrials. Did you ever give a thought to the possibility that maybe she was a 'Friendly'? That's something for you to think about, Joseph. Not all beings that are guides are from your earth. The universe is grand; there are many masters and many teachers to go around. We are all a part of God. The creator made all in His image; He is a being of Light.

A Word from Joseph

I can see now that I was put on my journey's path since I was a child. It is time for me to be that promoter of God that I was ordained to be! For years, the Collective have been preparing me to channel the Master Guide. Now it's time for the Ancient One to be heard and teach the words to be given by God.

God is the Creator of many Universes,
Earth is not Alone
Indigo

The Ancient One

Chapter Nineteen

Welcome Joseph, Welcome. We are here to make you aware of Who is and always was the *I Am*. The *I Am* is what *I Am*, all light bodies are all *I Am*; everything that exists is *I Am*. The *I Am* is of love and harmony and it is of power and thought. The *I Am* is of you and me and is of everything that is created. The universe is of One; and the One created all. The *I Am* is what *I Am*. Yes, Joseph, *I Am* that *I Am*! Remember these words and do not be afraid to use them. ***I Am* God!**

Why is it so hard for the inhabitants of earth to say the words, "*I Am* God?" The Creator made you in His own image. If you are made in the image of the One, then aren't you a part of that image? If the One is made in God's image, then the One is God. So do not be afraid to say, *I Am* that *I Am*, What *I Am* is *I Am*. *I Am* God!

The bible was written in many short stories that were put together in one book. Many men wrote the messages found in the bible throughout a time period of sixteen thousand years. These men were known as prophets

175

and, like you, Joseph, they had the gift to channel God's thoughts into words. They were the mediums who prophesized future spiritual events.

There were many mentors who were sent by God to help the souls on earth find true enlightenment. Moses and Joshua were sent to free a nation from bondage. Jehovah channeled to Moses the Commandments for all the people of *I Am* to follow. Jehovah is the Hebrew name for God. Moses had the people fear Jehovah in order for them to respect Jehovah. When Moses' mission was finished, the people of *I Am* were free. He handed his walking staff to Joshua instructing him to leave the wilderness and lead the people to the Promised Land. *"The Lord our God will guide you to the final resting place where our people will multiply and toil the riches of this sacred place."*

God clothed his only son, Jesus, in flesh so that the people of *I Am* would know how they were to sacrifice and be one with God. Jesus carried with Him the new teachings of Jehovah. He taught the people that Jehovah was our Father and He was sent by our Father to teach of love. Jesus was the true Son of God, the Son of the Father.

"Our Father God comes in love, not hate. We should not fear God, but embrace Him, for He is love. All is created in our Father's image. The human soul is as perfect as our Father God. We will dwell in our Father's Kingdom of the souls and our eternal life shall never end."

God, The Father, is of Spirit. The *I Am* is an energy that is stronger than any source there is. We look at life at different levels. The *I Am* is at the top and can never be equal to anyone. The Son, who is the Christ, is the Light of God from which all things were made. And the Holy Spirit is the life force of God; it's the energy that is channeled to everyone.

There are no other Gods. The *I Am* is the One and only true God. He is merciful, forgiving, kind and generous. There are many religions of different faiths and beliefs; however we all worship the one God. Beware of false religions; these are the religions that claim their teachings are God's teachings and *only through their ways* will you be one with God. God understands the love of his children who represent his teachings. God encourages those who wish to give thanks to those who directed the way to enlightenment. Great tasks were given to Moses, Joshua and Jesus.

As when the prophets wrote the bible, new messages are now being channeled to people who are called the Messengers of God. These people are

God's messengers for the coming New Age. Jesus called them his 'little flock'. They are the chosen ones to help The Christ prepare the beings of earth for the coming of Ascension. All will bear the mark of righteousness. They are on a mission for God to pave the way for all mankind. They will help the Christ in preparing the ones who are ready to come home to the Kingdom of Heaven; for it will be on earth as it is in heaven. Yes, the earth will ascend to the plane of radiant light. The ones who survive the transition will evolve into beings of Light, a reflection of God. All of the earth will dwell in His Kingdom.

The wicked shall perish; meaning that people of negative influence who are refusing to change their ways will not be permitted to reincarnate to the earth as evolved beings. They may stay with those who have crossed over and are part of the heavenly realm. When the time comes for them to reincarnate, they will fall to a place that resembles the third dimensional earth during its primitive stages, where temptation and negativity were a part of reality. Then it will be the time for those souls to live and reincarnate on their new world until all past karma has been fulfilled and the time for Ascension befall them.

Those who have crossed over are welcome, for they are ascended beings. Loved ones who have crossed over in the past and the ones who will cross during the transition will be a part of the New Earth. Other realities that aren't of the earth are now in tune to the new vibrations and will come. New lessons are to be learned along with a new way of life.

Joseph, you are one of the chosen ones out of the righteous many whose mission is to pave the way for the grand gathering of God's children. You have received the gift to channel in order to fulfill your mission. These gifts of God are not to be taken for granted. You are to educate the eluded and help the suffering. You must not let the temptation of ego interfere with our work. You are needed to minister to the people, for they are afraid of the unknown. You are to teach them about our Father and to help them discover their purpose here on earth. A messenger you will be, a messenger of God! It is a great task that's ahead of you, but one that will be filled with love and joy.

Information will come to you in thought and form. Use this to enlighten and enrich the mind, body and soul. New manuscript information will come. This new material will be of the New Age; it will pertain to the new law and order which will be in effect. These will be the New Commandments of

God's laws. Now go out among those who will listen and let them know that "The Christ" is here now, and for all eternity!

Joseph, you know me as the Ancient One. It is time for you to truly go within and feel the vibrations of who *I Am*. In the beginning of the earth's creations, God said, ***"Let there be Light!"*** And so it is, the Light of Christ brings in the life force to create the Earth and the Universe. The Light of Christ dwells within me to assist God in the birth of your universe. This is a part of who *I Am*.

When Jehovah created the first Adam, he clothed 'The Christ Consciousness' in flesh, to witness and glorify the beauty of the earth. This is a part of who *I Am*. Jehovah in Hebrew stands for 'God' and the words '*I Am*' mean 'God within'. The name "Joshua" in Hebrew is identical with the name "Jesus" in Greek.

Both Joshua and Jesus symbolize the divinity within man. Joshua and Jesus were derived from the word "Jehovah" which means *I Am That I Am*. His Hebrew name is "Yehoshua" and is known as "Joshua"; the descendant of the great national hero, "Joseph." Jesus the man was a descendant of Joseph, son of Jacob, a carpenter, by trade, in Galilee. What do these two great men have in common? They shared the Christ Consciousness. This is why we are known as the voice of *I Am*.

The Christ force incarnated in Joshua to free the people of *I Am*. A man of war; his strength was to lead his armies into hostile lands, to conquer and search for the Promised Land. Joshua is a part of who *I Am*. His Hebrew name is "Yeshua", and in Greek he is known as Jesus, The Christ, who was the opposite of Yehoshua; embodied in the flesh, so men would witness the glory of God. He was a man of peace and of love. Jesus embraced life and shared all of what he could give. Both men were messengers of the *I Am*. They both shared the Christ Consciousness; they are of The Christ. This is a part of who *I Am*.

So Joseph, you asked who I am? *I Am* **the Christ!** I Am the light of The Christ who created the universe; the Christ that was part of the first Adam, and the Christ that dwelled in Yehoshua and Yeshua. The Words of God come through me, and through the Christ all acts will come forth. I bring this message to all; these are the words of our beloved God. *I Am* **That** *I Am!*

~May the Lord Bless you and protect you~ The Ancient

The I Am is What I Am
The Ancient

Words from the Collective

Remember what the Christ is - it is the Life Force that is created and directed by God. God used the Christ Force to create the universe and all things; it is the Light where all things are made. When God created the Earth, he clothed the Christ Force in flesh and called it Adam. God did this to witness and glorify the beauty of the Earth through Adam. The Christ Force is universal; it is the force that created the Earth.

Sparrow Hawk is a vibration of the Christ Force and shares the same vibrations of the Earth. He was created to keep Law and Order and he was assigned to Earth as a protector. This is his part of the Grand Design of Creation.

Welcome - *I Am* Sparrow Hawk! Remember that all beings are related, meaning we are all from the One, The *I Am*. The Earth, Moon and Stars are created by the One. The One is the Great Spirit and all-powerful. Listen to the wisdom of the Great Spirit, He is in the wind; He is our Father, as the Earth is our Mother. Give her the respect she deserves and she will give you life! The animals were the first to take breath and multiply upon the Earth. She favors these creatures as the true beings of earth; she asks for humans to respect and treat them with kindness. I, Sparrow Hawk, request that all humans please take care of our Mother. She will not be able to withstand any more punishment from you. I am Earth's Protector and will not permit any more harm to her! Open your minds and feel the pain she has been put through in the last century.

I Am Sparrow Hawk, Protector of Mother Earth!

The Force of God is directed to all that exist. The Christ Force creates all levels of life and dwells among every living thing. When one is opened to this force, they have connected to the universe. The beings of Indigo help to direct the Christ Force to the beings who are now awakening to this force.

Good day, it is I, Indigo! Remember that the universe is all connected to the One. The *I Am* created all that there is. One day we will meet as light bodies and you will discover how one feels to be God. We are of the Christ and our energies are of many colors. If you look into a prism of multiple colors, you will witness the true ascended beings of the Indigo people. Our species is the foundation for the Light, meaning we can project the Christ

Force to where it is needed. This is how we are connected to the Christ Force; we direct the Light to where it needs to travel. We were the ones to direct the Light to Joseph for his awakening.

~ *Good Day to you and God Bless ~ Indigo*

The Messengers of the Christ are the ones to inform and educate about God and all that there is. To create an awakening for this is why Patrick and Genevieve were sent to Joseph. Patrick helps Joseph to lift his vibrations to connect with the Collective. And Genevieve was the one to express the love we feel for Joseph for the work he is about to perform.

Greetings everyone, it is Patrick! Don't forget that laughter raises the vibrations.

It has been a pleasure to be a part of this book and of Joseph's journeys. A little over a century ago, I was ascended into a Light Being. I was a Messenger for the Christ on the earth, as Joseph is in this century. Now I come through Joseph in his thoughts.

Remember that heaven is the astral plane; it is called the place for learning. Do not be deceived; it is not beyond the stars and moon, it is just a breath away. If you whisper, we will be able to hear you. The Kingdom of Heaven is now for all to see. Through the Force of Christ, we will enter into our Father's Kingdom. Learn to truly go within, for this is where we will find our Father God.

~ *The blessing of God on you ~Patrick*

And we cannot forget **Genevieve**, nor the love she feels for Joseph and the work she has bestowed. She is Joseph's Guardian Angel and knows him well. A few words she would like to express before we end this book:

> *The time has come for all mankind to end anger and hate*
> *We must have love and harmony as our final fate*
> *You must choose a path, the final path,*
> *which will amend your mistakes*
> *A quest for wisdom and fortune will be yours*
> *beyond heaven's gates*

It's a wonderful feeling to be a part of your earth once more. The warmth of the sun, and the smell of a rose is what I was craving; the taste of honey on my lips, and the feel of mountain dew. Your vibrations are what I desire, and to be a part of you. Hello, I am Genevieve and I am an Angel. We have finally connected to Joseph, so it would not be fair to say, "goodbye." So instead, we will say, "hello", until we meet again!

~ All of my love to all of the people now and forever ~ Genevieve

A Final Note from Joseph

"To Remain on Guard, to be a Watcher... To be a Wonderful Reporter! This is your purpose. For you will be proof, and always have been proof, in the past, of the Christ."

This was the message I received from Marilyn's guide, Gene, back in 1994. When I received the message, I thought I was to be a messenger for Jesus. As the years passed, the name Yehoshua, along with Yeshua, was constantly imprinted into my mind, but I was confused about who 'the Ancient' was who seemed to want to communicate with me. When I found out that Yeshua was the name for Jesus in Hebrew, I thought that maybe Jesus was the Ancient One.

Needless to say, many doubts entered my mind as to why this great man would choose *me* to be a messenger. My wife, Lisa, set me straight by reminding me about Marilyn's message that I had been a reporter for the Christ and also about Deborah's message from the Bejianes that I was on an important mission. I would be channeling manuscript information pertaining to the Christ.

So who is the Ancient? If it isn't Yeshua, than it must be Yehoshua! Eventually I realized that they were one and the same. Jesus was Joshua in a past life and in both lives, the Christ force dwelled in them.

Now I have clarity. The Ancient One is the Christ Force. It is the Life Force of God who will channel information to me. It was ten years ago when I first connected to the Collective. During that time, I lived my life and did what I had to do to fulfill my karma. I'm at a time in my life where I need to devote more of my time to the Collective and to be that Promoter of God I was ordained to be. I will begin to work on the new manuscript, practice my channeling and continue to help people connect with their loved ones that have crossed over. I will also focus on using my psychic abilities.

When you are a Channel, you must dedicate much time to meditation. I must practice and learn to be the best that I can be. I must conquer the fears and doubts that limit me. I hope one day that my channeling will help bring peace and harmony to mankind. Thank you for being a part of my journey and I'll see you on the continuation of *Our Never Ending Journey of Life!*

~ Love and many Blessings ~Joseph

Final Words of the Collective

We would like to thank readers for allowing the wisdom of truth to be expressed. The knowledge that was foretold in this book was given by beings of the Collective. We come to you from all parts of the universe to express wisdom and truth of the *I Am*, for the *I Am* is the Creator of all things.

We will leave off for now in this journey of *Is There More to Life Than What We Know?* and continue with new writings of Our Never Ending Journey of Life in future books. There are many Masters and Teachers of the Collective. Joseph will tap into this beautiful source of truth and teach the lessons to you. It may seem that we are at the end - or maybe it's just the beginning - of our journey in life. However, if life is never ending, then there is no beginning or end, just continuation!

~God Bless You ~ The Collective

The Glossary

Adam: the first man in the Bible created by God.

Angel: a divine being who acts as a messenger of God.

Apparitions: an appearance of a supposed ghost or something ghostly.

Ascension: spiritually enlightened beings, once mere mortals, who have undergone a process of spiritual transformation.

Astral Body: a second body, not directly perceivable by the human senses, believed to co-exist with and survive the death of the physical body, the Spirit.

Astral Plane: a level of existence where the Spirit goes between death and entry into the spirit world.

Astral Projection: the ability to send the astral body, the spirit, outside of the physical body while both remain connected.

Astral Travel: the ability to send the astral body, the spirit, outside of the physical body while both remain connected; the astral body travels to another place.

Astrological Age: a time period in astrology that is believed to cause major changes in the Earth's inhabitant's development. It roughly corresponds to the time taken for the vernal equinox to move through one of the twelve constellations of the zodiac. The Ages in astrology, however, do not correspond to the actual constellation boundaries where the vernal equinox may be occurring in a given time.

Astrological Signs: the twelve signs in the Zodiac calendar. ♒ Aquarius (Water Bearer): Jan. 20–Feb 18 ♓ Pisces (Fish): Feb. 19–March 20 ♈ Aries (Ram): March 21–April 19 ♉ Taurus (Bull): April 20–May 20 ♊ Gemini (Twins): May 21–June 20 ♋ Cancer (Crab): June 21–July 22 ♌ Leo (Lion): July 23–Aug. 22 ♍ Virgo (Virgin): Aug. 23–Sept. 22 ♎ Libra (Scales): Sept. 23–Oct. 22 ♏ Scorpio (Scorpion): Oct. 23–Nov. 21 ♐ Sagittarius (Archer): Nov. 22–Dec. 21 ♑ Capricorn (Goat): Dec. 22–Jan. 19

Astrological Zodiac: a zodiac that divides the ecliptic into twelve astrological signs of equal length.

Atlantis: described as the greatest of all historical mysteries. Plato, writing about 350 BCE, was the first to speak of the great island in the Atlantic Ocean which had vanished "in a day and a night," and been submerged beneath the waves of the Atlantic.

Atlantians: People who lived on Atlantis.

Atonement: the making of reparation for a sin or a mistake.

Attunement: to become receptive or responsive to vibration frequency.

Awakening: a sudden recognition or realization of enlightenment.

Aura: a force that surrounds all people and objects, often discernible as a colorful glow.

Awareness: mindful that God exists because you realize that God is all that there is.

Baptism: a religious ceremony in which someone is sprinkled with or immersed in water to symbolize purification.

Being ness: the state of existing, a living thing, especially one conceived of as supernatural or not living on earth.

Bejianes: pronounced (Ba-gee-ins) a race of beings of a higher dimension than earth. They are a part of the Christ Consciousness. The Bejianes are here to help the human race of earth to find their original blueprint code and to find their true-self, and also to ensure them enlightenment.

Bible: considered the sacred book of the Christian religion and the Hebrew Scriptures, the sacred book of the Jewish religion.

Biblical: relating to the Bible, or written about in the Bible.

Brotherhood: the spiritual members of a collective force working as one thought that teachings are of God.

Buddha: somebody who has achieved a state of perfect enlightenment.

Buddhism: a world religion or philosophy based on the teaching of the Buddha and holding that suppressing worldly desires can attain a state of enlightenment.

Carnal: relating to or consisting of the body, physical needs or appetites, especially as contrasted with spiritual or intellectual qualities.

Celestial Sphere: an imaginary rotating sphere of "gigantic radius", concentric and co-axial with the Earth. All objects in the sky can be thought of as lying upon the sphere. Projected, from their corresponding geographic equivalents, are the celestial equator and the celestial poles. The celestial sphere projection is a very practical tool for positional astronomy.

Circle of Life: where all life begins. Living things all have a moment at which they become "alive." That beginning of life marks the first point on the circle of life. Each family of living things has its own life cycle.

Clairaudient: the psychic ability to hear beyond the range of the normal human hearing.

Claircognizance translates to "clear knowingness"; this is an ability to just know things without conventional sensory input; no one tells you, you just *know* it.

Clairsentient: clear feeling - to feel the emotions and personalities of the deceased.

Clairvoyance: the psychic ability to see things beyond the range of normal human vision.

Chakra: in yoga, any one of the energy centers of spiritual power in the body.

Channeling: in spiritualism, the practice of acting as a medium for receiving messages from the spirit world, Guides, Teachers and Masters of God's laws.

Christ: in the beginning of the earth creations God said, "Let There Be Light!" And so it is, the Light of Christ brings in the life force to create the Earth and the Universe. This energy was a part of the Master called Jesus, for this is why he was known as The Christ.

Christ Consciousness: beings made up and in tune with the Christ Energy. This energy is a very high vibration with God.

Christ Energy: See Christ Vibration.

Christ Vibration: is the Son, the right hand of God; its highest level to be with God.

Collective: a Brotherhood of Spirit Guides of the Christ Conscience working as one thought that teachings are of God and the Christ Vibrations.

Consciousness: the state of being awake and aware of what is going on around you.

Consecrated: to officially make something holy and able to be used for religious ceremonies.

Cosmic Year: 129,600 calendar years represent one cosmic year

Crossing Over: the end of a life and the crossing into the afterlife.

Dark Side: fall from grace, the Fallen Angel or Devil, the negative vibration of energy.

Dimension: a level of consciousness, existence, or reality.

Dream: a sequence of images that appear involuntarily to the mind of a sleeping person, often a mixture of real and imaginary characters, places, and events.

Dvapara Yuga: the third age out of four in a Yuga.

Elijah: a messenger from God in the first half of the ninth century BC

Elizabeth: means in Hebrew "Worshiper of God." wife of Zachary and mother of John the Baptist,

Energy: the capacity of a body to bring God's Force.

Enlightened: having achieved the realization of a spiritual understanding, especially when it results in the transcendence of human suffering and desire, having the clarity that God is all there is.

Enlightened Path: the journey you travel to achieve the realization of a spiritual understanding, especially when results in the transcendence of human suffering and desire, having the clarity that God is all there is.

Entity: the state of having existence.

E.S.P: (extrasensory perception) most commonly called the "sixth sense"- sensory information that an individual receives which comes beyond the ordinary five senses; sight, hearing, smell, taste, and touch. E.S.P. can provide the individual with information of the present, past, and future; as it seems to originate in a second, or alternate reality.

Etheric State: everything in physical reality exists in two states, the physical state and the etheric state. Physical matter and its etheric double co-exist in the same space-time but out of phase with each other on two different planes of reality. Anti-matter is the etheric double of physical matter.

Existence: all living things.

Extraterrestrial: existing or coming from somewhere outside the Earth and its atmosphere.

Father: in the Christian religion, God, especially when considered as the first person of the Holy Trinity; Farther, Son, and Holy Ghost.

Father's Kingdom: the kingdom of God: Heaven.

Free Will: the ability to act or make choices as a free and autonomous being and not solely as a result of compulsion or predestination.

Galactic Humans: the fiber of your being is similar to those that resided on the earth thousands of years ago. Your brothers reside as a higher vibration than earth. They are from parts of the universe you are not aware of, at this time and space. These humans that we speak of are your ancestors. You are created in the same mold as God created them.

Grays: a race from the dark side; prone to subject creatures on earth subject to their experiments. They have small gray bodies that stand around four feet tall with large heads and black, almond-shaped eyes. The Grays are more technologically advanced than the third dimensional human race. They are invaders of Earth.

Great Spirit: the all-powerful, all-knowing Creator of the universe,

Ghost: the spirit of someone who has died, supposed to appear as a shadowy form, or cause sounds or the movement of objects.

God: the Being believed in monotheistic religions such as Judaism, Islam, and Christianity to be the all-powerful, all-knowing Creator of the universe, worshipped as the only God.

God's Energy: God's Life force.

God's Life Force: the Light of God from which everything was made.

Godlike: having the qualities and the goodness to be in God's Image.

Golden Age: the time of enlightenment.

Grand Conjunction: a simultaneous occurrence of events, the convergence of the New Age, the Cosmic Year and Golden Age.

Guardian Angel: an angel that looks after a particular individual.

Harmonic Convergence: this event only happens around twenty-four thousands years. This day will welcome the coming of the New Age. It will unite people to pray for peace and the healing of the earth, and raise our Vibration.

Heaven: a place of supreme happiness and peace where our soul goes after death, the dwelling place of God.

Higher Self: your soul located at a higher plane than your spirit on earth that is the part of you known as the lower self.

Hinduism: the religion of India and the oldest of the worldwide religions, characterized by a belief in reincarnation and the essential unity of forms and theories.

Holistic: including or involving all of something, especially all of somebody's physical, mental, and social conditions, not just physical symptoms, in the treatment of illness.

Holy Spirit: in Christianity, the third person of the Trinity, understood as the spiritual force of God.

Hypnotherapy: the use of hypnosis in treating illness, for example, in dealing with physical pain or psychological problems.

I AM: the Being believed in monotheistic religions such as Christianity and Judaism, to be the all-powerful, all-knowing Creator of the universe, worshipped as the only God.

Illusion: something that deceives the senses or mind, for example, by appearing to exist when it does not or appearing to be one thing when it is in fact another.

Immanuel: the Messiah, referred to in Jewish and Christian scriptures, whom Christians believe to be Jesus Christ.

Indigo: one of the Collective, Joseph's control, teacher and Inner Voice; possessed with healing abilities.

Intuition: something known or believed instinctively, without actual evidence for it.

Jehovah: the being believed in monotheistic religions such as Judaism, to be the all-powerful all-knowing Creator of the universe, worshipped as the only God.

Jesus: his name in Aramaic is Yeshua and was known as Jesus of Nazareth, the man from Galilee who became known as Jesus the Christ.

John the Harbinger: (John the Baptist) a cousin to Jesus ordained to proclaim the arrival of the Savior. Known for conducting baptisms, the rite of cleansing; those who are cleansed, shall become the son of purity, and they shall be forgiven.

Joseph : chosen by God to be Jesus' father on earth. God knew that Jesus would need a foster father to raise him and teach him. The Bible tells us that he was a "just man." That means he was a good man, honest, fair, and God-loving.

Joshua: his original Hebrew name is Yehoshua. The name Josuha is identical with the name "Jesus" in Greek. Both Joshua and Jesus symbolize the divinity within man. Joshua's and Jesus' names were derived from the word "Jehovah", which means I Am That I Am.

Journey of Life: the journey of the spirit within an individual person in life.

Kali Yuga: the age of darkness, it's one of the four stages of development that the world goes through as part of the cycle of Yugas.

Karma: the word Karma means the total effect of a person's actions and conduct during successive phases of their existence. Another way to look at Karma is that it stands for cause and effect; what goes around comes around.

Kirlian Photography: Semyon Kirlian discovered accidentally that when a metal plate is subjected to a high-voltage electric field, an image is created on the plate. The image looks like a colored halo or coronal discharge. This image is the physical manifestation of the spiritual aura, or "life force", which surrounds each living thing.

Kristo: from the Greek word "Kristos", that is the Christ and means the "Anointed". It is the same definition of the Hebrew word, "Messiah".

Kundalini: a Sanskrit word meaning either "coiled up" or "coiling like a snake." An awakening and spiritual maturation.

Levels: a plane or of existence; of spiritual achievement.

Lower Self: your spirit that is the part of you on earth connected to your Higher Self, which is your Soul located in a higher plane than earth.

Mary: Mother of Jesus; Mary, a virgin, learned from the angel Gabriel that she would conceive Jesus through the Holy Spirit.

Mary of Magdalene: appears with more frequency than other women in the canonical Gospels and is shown as being a close follower of Jesus. Mary's presence at the Crucifixion and Jesus' tomb, while hardly conclusive, is at least consistent with the role of grieving wife and widow.

Materialism: devotion to material wealth and possessions at the expense of spiritual or intellectual values.

Master Guide: the main guide to bring in spiritual information.

Matrix: a situation or set of circumstances that allows or encourages the origin, development, or the growth of spirituality.

Mayan Calendar: a system of distinct calendars and almanacs used by the Maya civilization of pre-Columbian Mesoamerica.

Medicine Wheel: a Native American physical manifestation of Spiritual energy. It is a wheel of protection and enables us to gather surrounding energies into a focal point and to commune with Spirit, Self and Nature (ALL elemental forces of Creation)!

Mediums: people who have a special gift that allows the spirit to give messages from the afterlife. The objective of a medium's work is to prove survival of the human personality after death and to help the bereaved come to terms with their loss. Sittings with mediums are not for fortune-telling, but are sessions to provide evidence of survival. Medium-ship uses no aids (such as tarot) or interpretative skills. A Mediumistic Reading is a direct intuitive link with the spirit world, with the objective to give proof that our loved ones and we survive physical death.

Meditate: to empty the mind of thoughts, or concentrate the mind on one thing, in order to develop the mind and spirit.

Mentality: a habitual way of thinking or interpreting events peculiar to an individual or type of person, especially with reference to the behaviors that it produces.

Messenger: is a courier of God's messages delivered to humanity.

Messiah: in Christianity, Jesus Christ is regarded as the Messiah, He was prophesied in the Hebrew Bible as an anointed King who would lead the Jews back to the land of Israel and establish justice in the world.

Metaphysical Science: a division of philosophy concerned with the fundamental nature of reality, including the study of the supernatural; spirit guides, ghosts, extraterrestrials and psychic phenomena.

Moses: a Hebrew prophet, and the brother of Aaron - led the Israelites from slavery in Egypt to the Promised Land and was the deliverer of the Ten Commandments.

Native American: a member of any of the indigenous people of North, South, or Central America, belonging to the Mongoloid groups of people.

Negative Force: the opposite of the Light, turning way from God.

New Age: relating to a cultural movement dating from the 1980s that emphasizes spiritual consciousness and often involves belief in reincarnation and astrology and the practice of meditation, vegetarianism, and holistic medicine.

Reincarnation: the cyclical return of a soul to live another life in a new body.

Past Life Progression: about making mind/body/spirit progress in this life based on the remembered experiences of other incarnations. It is not about 'karmic' payback for 'bad' past lives, as all lives are important parts in the development of the Whole Self.

Past Life Regression: (PLR) if one is reincarnated in this lifetime, this is the journeying into one's past lives, witnessing the events of their past lives.

Patrick: one of the Collective that brings in laughter to lift the vibrations to connect with the Collective. Patrick brings the teachings of Christ and Heaven.

Pineal gland: its location deep in the brain seems to indicate its importance. This combination led to its being a "mystery" gland with myth, superstition and even metaphysical theories surrounding its perceived function.

Pendulum: a weight hung from a fixed point so that it can swing freely back and forth under the influence of gravity. Allows for connection with one's subconscious thought or with spirit

Phenomenon: somebody or something that is - or is considered to be - truly extraordinary and marvelous.

Physical: relating to the body, rather than with the mind, the soul, or the feelings.

Plane: a level or of existence, of spiritual achievement.

Prophet: someone who foretells the future.

Psychic: is someone with second sight - ESP (Extra Sensory Perception.) Some psychics use tools such as Tarot Cards, Runes, Playing Cards or Palmistry. A psychic may also 'read' a person's aura - the energy field that surrounds living things. They use their psychic gifts together with their interpretation skills and knowledge of divination. This gives insight into the inquirer's past, present and potential future.

Psychic Medium: is someone who works both as a psychic and as a medium. All true mediums have psychic abilities, so the term Psychic Medium is a somewhat misleading term. All Mediums are Psychic.

Psychometry: the alleged ability to obtain information about a person or event by touching an object related to that person or event.

Resurrection: the rising of Jesus Christ from the dead, after his crucifixion and entombment.

Rebirth: the revival of important ideas or forces, usually as part of broad and significant change.

Reiki: a treatment in alternative medicine in which healing energy is channeled from the practitioner to the patient to enhance energy and reduce stress, pain, and fatigue.

Sacred Tree: the branches are all Nations. The branches grow in all directions, to the North and South, to the East and West. This connects all humans together on earth. The branches that point to the heavens will bring the Universe - the Great Spirit!

Satya Yuga: when humankind is governed by God and every manifestation or work is close to the purest ideal, and mankind will allow intrinsic goodness to rule supreme. It is sometimes referred to as the "Golden Age."

Scribe: a person who copies or writes documents, especially someone who copied manuscripts, the Torah and other religious documents using a quill pen on parchment.

Séance: a meeting during which a spiritualist attempts to receive communications from the spirits of the dead.

Seer: someone who is able to see into the future.

Shaman: someone who acts as a go-between for the physical and spiritual realms, and who is said to have particular powers such as prophesy and healing.

Soul: it's your Higher Self and an image and all-knowledge of God; the spirit part of a human being that continues to exist after the body dies.

Soul Evolution: the spiritual growth of the Soul.

Sparrow Hawk: one of the Collective, the Protector of Mother Earth, Universal Energy.

Spirit: supernatural being that does not have a physical body, for example; a ghost, or an angel.

Spirit Guides: ascended masters are a group of spiritually enlightened beings, once mere mortals, who have undergone a process of spiritual transformation. According to these teachings, they remain attentive to the spiritual needs of humanity and act as superintendents of its spiritual growth.

Spirituality: not synonymous with religion. Different world religions have proposed various doctrines and belief systems about the nature of a God and humanity's relationship with it. Spirituality, on the other hand, refers to the common experience behind these various points of view.

Spiritual Healers: the channeling of healing energy from its spiritual source to someone who needs it is called spiritual healing. The channel is usually a person, whom called a healer, and the healing energy is usually transferred to the patient through the healer's hands. The healing does not come from the healer, but through him.

Star Child: spirits not from the earth but other galaxies or universes who want to experience life on earth.

Supernatural: relating or attributed to phenomena that cannot be explained by natural laws.

Tetra Yuga: is known as the Silver Age. Spiritual awareness had decreased and some men had parted from God. Materialism is what was important to some. A few spiritual minds became lost and the physical reality became what was real.

The Light: the God Force, the Christ, in which all things are made.

Trumpet: an instrument used by mediums; it's used for spirits to communicate by voice through the cone.

Trance: the state of apparent semi-unconsciousness that a spiritual medium enters into, in an attempt to communicate with the dead.

Trance Channeling: the state of apparent semi-unconsciousness in spiritualism, the practice used by a medium for receiving messages and expressions from the spirit world.

UFO: Unidentified Flying Object, a flying object that cannot be identified and is thought by some to be an alien spacecraft.

Universe: the totality of all matter and energy that exists in the vastness of space, whether known to human beings or not.

Universal: relating to the universe or everything.

Universal Commandments: God's Laws for all beings of the Universe.

Universal Life Force: the Life Force of God.

Universal Energy: the same as Universal Life Force.

Vernal Equinox: the equinox happens when the Sun is at one of two opposite points, on the celestial sphere, where the celestial equator and ecliptic intersect. In a wider sense, the equinoxes are the two days each year when the center of the Sun spends an equal amount of time above and below the horizon at every location on Earth.

Vibration: The movement of electrons and protons of every atom, every molecule, every substance, creates vibration.

Wisdom: accumulated knowledge of life, or in a particular sphere of activity that has been gained through experience.

Yehoshua: the name of Joshua in Hebrew.

Yeshua: is Jesus' name in Hebrew.

Yuga: in Hinduism, any one of the four stages in each cycle of history, each worse than the one before.

Zacharias: is the father to John the Baptist.

Zodiac: a chart linking twelve constellations to twelve divisions of the year, used as the astrologer's main tool for analyzing character and predicting the future.

9 780595 434497